Lead
Improvement.

A Personal & Organizational Journey

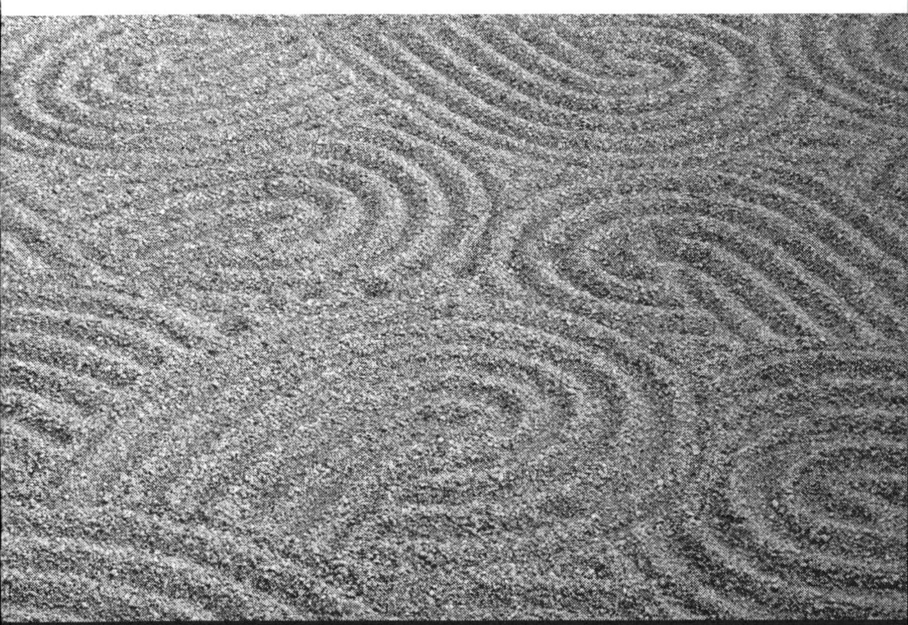

Aaron Fausz, William Kirkwood, Blair Warman Nickle,
& Maureen Sullivan

ISBN: 978-0-578-21299-9

Dedication

We dedicate this book to W. Terry Howell. Terry has been a mentor, coach, counselor, colleague, and friend to us for many years. He has been a driving force behind much of our personal and professional lives, including this book. His insights and anecdotes have increased our knowledge, his encouragement has provided needed inspiration, and his constructive feedback has made us better people.

Contents

Preface

This book is an attempt to synthesize our collective and accumulated learning. It is based on our experiences—what has worked and what has not—as well as what we have learned from our amazing customers and colleagues. This book also integrates the theories of W. Edwards Deming and Ken Wilber. Much has been written about each of these complementary theories, but to our knowledge this book is the first attempt to integrate these different perspectives into a unified whole to gain new insights into leadership effectiveness. More on the work of these two great thinkers can be found in the section "Standing on the Shoulders of Giants."

We intend this work to be a practical yet thought-provoking guide to help leaders achieve and sustain lasting improvement at both the personal and organizational levels. The topics discussed are agnostic with regard to a specific improvement methodology. Like many healthcare leaders, we have survived the past few decades' alphabet soup of process improvement methodologies including QI, TQM, CQI, Six Sigma, and Lean. We incorporate what we have learned from all of these approaches to deploy not just an improvement *method* but an improvement *system*. Regardless of the improvement approach you prefer, the information in this book will be relevant and helpful for your improvement journey.

We authors come from different professional fields, and our paths have crossed at different times and places across many years. Two of us chose healthcare as an early calling while two stumbled into it by chance and good fortune. One of us was a clinician, providing care directly to patients. One of us was a hospital administrator. Two of us came through organizational development and learning roles. Despite these differences, which we view as strengths, we are united in the goal of helping healthcare leaders understand and apply the concepts in this book. We believe these ideas can sharpen the acuity with which healthcare leaders examine and improve themselves as well as their organizations.

Part 1: The Context

Standing on the Shoulders of Giants

The Latin phrase *nanos gigantum humeris insidentes* translates as *dwarfs standing on the shoulders of giants.* In a letter to Robert Hooke in 1675, Sir Isaac Newton famously said, "If I have seen further it is by standing on the shoulders of giants." We would be remiss if we failed to acknowledge some of the intellectual giants who have inspired us over the years and upon whose shoulders we stand. The most significant of these people are honored below and in the "Influencers" section at the end of the book.

Two people stand apart from the others because of the profound influence they have had in shaping us. These are the tallest of the giants whose thinking and teachings combine to provide the underlying framework for this book: W. Edwards Deming and Ken Wilber.

W. Edwards Deming was an American engineer, statistician, professor, author, lecturer, and management consultant. He is best known for his work to revitalize the industry and economy of Japan after World War II. Many in Japan credit Deming as a primary catalyst for the post-war Japanese economic miracle of the 1950s. During this period, Japan rose from the ashes of war to become the second largest economy in the world. Japanese business leaders accomplished their remarkable turnaround through the core ideas Deming taught. Those ideas included the following:

- Better design of products
- Production of consistent and high-quality products

- Improvement of processes, products, and services through experimentation and the study of data

Deming is best known in the United States for his 14 Points and his System of Profound Knowledge®, both of which were introduced in his book, *Out of the Crisis* (Deming 1986). The System of Profound Knowledge® includes four fields of study that Deming deemed critical for effective leadership and management:

1. Appreciation for a system (systems thinking)
2. Understanding of variation (statistical thinking)
3. A theory of knowledge (the scientific method)
4. Some knowledge of psychology (particularly regarding motivation)

Deming saw these four components as the foundation upon which he built his 14 Points: his key principles for leaders to follow to significantly improve the effectiveness of an organization. Deming's principles are a combination of philosophy and programmatic ideas, and all relate to people directly or indirectly. All are transformational in nature. Because of their importance, we have included Deming's 14 Points (Deming 1986, 23).

Deming's 14 Points

1. Create constancy of purpose toward improvement of product and service, with the aim to become competitive and to stay in business, and to provide jobs.
2. Adopt the new philosophy. We are in a new economic age. Western management must awaken to the challenge, must learn their responsibilities, and take on leadership for change.
3. Cease dependence on inspection to achieve quality. Eliminate the need for inspection on a mass basis by building quality into the product in the first place.
4. End the practice of awarding business on the basis of price tag. Instead, minimize total cost. Move toward a single supplier for any one item, on a long-term relationship of loyalty and trust.

5. Improve constantly and forever the system of production and service, to improve quality and productivity, and thus constantly decrease costs.
6. Institute training on the job.
7. Institute leadership. The aim of supervision should be to help people and machines and gadgets to do a better job. Supervision of management is in need of overhaul, as well as supervision of production workers.
8. Drive out fear, so that everyone may work effectively for the company.
9. Break down barriers between departments. People in research, design, sales, and production must work as a team, to foresee problems of production and in use that may be encountered with the product or service.
10. Eliminate slogans, exhortations, and targets for the work force asking for zero defects and new levels of productivity. Such exhortations only create adversarial relationships, as the bulk of the causes of low quality and low productivity belong to the systems and thus lie beyond the power of the work force.
    a. Eliminate work standards (quotas) on the factory floor. Substitute leadership.
    b. Eliminate management by objective. Eliminate management by numbers, numerical goals. Substitute leadership.
11. Remove barriers that rob the hourly worker of his right to pride of workmanship. The responsibility of supervisors must be changed from sheer numbers to quality.
12. Remove barriers that rob people in management and in engineering of their right to pride of workmanship. This means, inter alia, abolishment of the annual or merit rating and of management by objective.
13. Institute a vigorous program of education and self-improvement.
14. Put everybody in the company to work to accomplish the transformation. The transformation is everybody's job.

Deming's ideas are timeless. He informed and shaped all subsequent quality improvement methodologies including total quality management (TQM), continuous quality improvement (CQI), Six Sigma, and Lean. His principles were in place long before any of these methodologies had names. To this day, our approach is guided in a large measure by the ideas and teachings of W. Edwards Deming.

The second giant among giants is Ken Wilber. Wilber is a philosopher and writer whose work integrates multiple fields of study into one single model or framework (Wilber 2016). Wilber's work on transpersonal psychology and his *Integral Theory* draw on research insights from across the world's greatest knowledge traditions including cultural studies, anthropology, systems theory, developmental psychology, biology, and spirituality.

Wilber's Integral Theory is a metatheory that attempts to explain how the various academic disciplines and forms of knowledge fit together cohesively. It is widely used in the study and practice of leadership. Wilber uses the word *integral* to mean to integrate, to bring together, to join, to link, and to embrace. His work is elegant and worthy of exploration. For a deeper dive into Integral Theory we encourage you to explore Wilber's many books.

Wilber's Integral Theory model (Figure 1) provides an accessible framework to explore personal development and organizational improvement. The model is constructed on a four-quadrant grid along the axes of internal–external and individual–collective. In the context of leading organizational improvement, each of the four interdependent dimensions provides a perspective on our leadership experience and current reality. Each quadrant is worthy of contemplation.

	Internal	*External*
Individual	Values, beliefs, priorities, and motivation of the individual.	Actions and behaviors of the individual
Collective	Values and beliefs of the collective	Actions and behaviors of the collective

Figure 1: Ken Wilber's Integral Theory model provides an accessible framework to explore personal and organizational improvement.

- **Internal-Individual perspective**
  The upper-left quadrant interprets and focuses on one's personal internal values, beliefs, and hidden maps or mindsets. These mindsets form our internal operating system, akin to a computer's internal operating system. Wilber offers that personal exploratory work within this dimension is a form of *waking up*. Deep personal change comes from the process of recognizing the mindsets that trigger our behaviors. This is where we as leaders look inward at our purpose, values, and meaning in our work. This is our interior work.

- **External-Individual perspective**
  The upper-right quadrant interprets and focuses on the actions of the individual as seen by others. It is within this dimension that mindsets manifest themselves in behaviors visible to oth-

ers, though not always to ourselves. This quadrant encourages us to seek feedback from others so that we become conscious of both our actions and our impact on others.

- **Internal-Collective perspective**
  The lower-left quadrant is where the interior of the group is defined. Within this dimension reside the group's values, norms, shared habits, and purpose. In other words, this is where organizational culture exists. Culture is the internal operating system for the group and larger organization. This powerful and self-sustaining system is evidenced through the outward behaviors or artifacts of the group yet, like the individual operating system noted above, it is not visible through casual observation. It is with deliberate awareness and work within the other three quadrants that the culture can be understood and shaped.

- **External-Collective perspective**
  The lower-right quadrant is the dimension where the exterior of the organization is defined. The exterior is visible in the systems, structures, workflow design, and workplace practices. This is the province of most organizational change initiatives as leaders seek influence and control over these business elements.

Each dimension of the model provides valuable insights in how leaders can develop themselves and improve their organizations. However, working on only one or two of these dimensions is not sufficient to realize the large-scale improvements organizations need. If we view our roles, behaviors, and approaches as leaders through only one or two of these dimensions, we create a fragmented approach to leading. It is the deep learning and development from each dimension integrated into a whole that generates new, robust leadership development and organizational improvement. By engaging in a thoughtful and purposeful application of this model, leaders can gain new wisdom that leads to personal development and organizational transformation.

In writing this book, we attempted to remain true to the teachings that flow from the work of both Deming and Wilber. These teachings emphasize the importance of individual responsibility; personal development; organizational improvement from a systems perspective; design of systems and structures that bring forth continual improvement; organizational cultures that respect the contributions of its members; and a determined focus to provide unparalleled care and service to our patients, families, and communities. We believe the synergy in their work creates a dynamic opportunity to explore and learn about ourselves as leaders and how we approach improving our organizations.

This book is not about beating the competition, increasing market capitalization, becoming first in some ranking, or racing from success to success. We know that our readers are likely aware of the current challenges confronting healthcare, and we will not reiterate those. Instead, this book is about helping leaders to better understand themselves and their organizations so they can fundamentally transform the healthcare industry. It is ultimately about improving patient outcomes while making higher-quality care more affordable. It is also about humanizing care and creating the best possible experiences for patients and healthcare team members. It is about providing meaningful jobs where people can contribute, grow, and find purpose. It is about shaping the healthcare industry to enable everyone to live happy and healthy lives.

We have purposefully organized the chapters of this book along Wilber's concept of the individual view (Part 2) and the collective view (Part 3). Wilber's internal (reflective) and external (behavioral) aspects, as well as Deming's teachings, are interwoven throughout.

There is one additional construct, a three-part perspective, that informs the book:

- Awareness
- Approach

- Action

In Parts 1 and 2, we delve into reflective disciplines that are intended to increase *awareness*. In Part 3, we offer various leadership *approaches* that enhance organizational improvement. Lastly, at the close of each chapter, we ask questions intended not only to increase *awareness* but also to encourage *action*. We suggest thoughtful contemplation of these questions. A bit of quiet reflection can often uncover intellectual and emotional reactions that bring great insight. We invite our readers to take time to ponder.

We did not intend the book to be something that is read once and put on a shelf. Although readers may choose to read it completely through once for a sense of the whole, the content is designed to be revisited over time as a companion in a leader's ongoing growth and development.

Finally, we recommend taking the perspective of a teacher as well as a learner. Read with the purpose of sharing and discussing key concepts with someone else. This mindset can aid in concept retention and increase the motivation to apply what is learned.

The consumer is
the most important point
on the production line.

—W. Edwards Deming (1986, 5)

The Heart of the Journey

But for the customer, why would we even be here?

> **Customer:** The person or organization receiving your products or services; the one who benefits from what you produce. In healthcare, the patient is our primary customer, but we have other customers as well. We serve the patients' family members and the broader community at large. We also serve internal customers: our colleagues and peers within our own organizations who depend on our work.

No one argues against a focus on the **customer**. What would the counter argument be? "By ignoring the customer, I can keep my head down and become singularly focused on my daily work life." This is not logical because, at some level, we all recognize that an organization without a customer is wasteful. A worker without a customer is adrift. Without a defined beneficiary of the products and services we produce, healthcare professionals serve no purpose or mission in society.

Many individual leaders and organizations talk about a customer-centric approach, but it is often just lip service: all talk and no action. Many healthcare organizations lack a rich and robust customer focus that is mobilized into action. True customer focus is more than words. It is more than a "We Love Our Customers" banner strung across the front door.

One way to consider how a *true* customer focus looks and feels is to contrast it with a *façade* of customer focus. This difference might be described as the difference between espoused values and values in action.

The following examples illustrate the shift from words to action.

FROM: Having a vague notion of who customers are and exhorting patient-centeredness

TO: Having clarity and intense focus on customers

A truly customer-focused organization has a clear, crisp, and sharp understanding of those who are being served. At every location in the organization, associates can call out with specificity those who use their products and services. This exactness and clarity applies to both internal and external customers. Customers have names and faces. They are concrete manifestations, not abstract concepts.

FROM: Being distant and disconnected

TO: Being present and in a relationship

It is possible to maintain a professional manner and yet still be in a relationship with the customer. In fact, it is only when team members are in a relationship with the customer that they can move from acting as if they care to really caring. It is only when team members are in relationships with customers that they take on the mantle of humble service. To be in a relationship with a customer means to see the world from the customer's perspective. It means to view it as a privilege to serve and not a burden. It means to have respect and compassion for the customer.

FROM: Conducting research and surveys

TO: Listening deeply to customers

Satisfaction surveys and customer service ratings are common throughout all industries, including healthcare. However, this form of customer research, if used singularly and in isolation, may actually be a barrier to what was described previously: the development of a true relationship with the customer. The survey becomes a way to know about the customer but not a way to know the customer.

That is not to say that surveys and traditional customer research have no value. They certainly do, but they are not sufficient to sustain deep, thoughtful, and responsive interactions with customers. That relationship comes only with dialogue: face-to-face, eye-to-eye conversation.

FROM: Acting as the expert

TO: Sharing and deferring to expertise

Healthcare is an expert industry. There is no doubt that the clinicians who spend their formative years on professional education and continue to keep up with professional advances have much to give to their customers. But the trap is that these clinicians, and indeed any highly trained and experienced professionals in any field, become viewed as experts rather than as having expertise.

What is the difference? The term expert implies an individual who has comprehensive and authoritative knowledge in a particular area or endeavor. In comparison, Karl Weick and Kathleen Sutcliffe, deep thinkers in the realm of highly reliable organizations, define *expertise* as "an assemblage of knowledge, experience, learning, and intuitions that is seldom embodied in a single individual" (Weick & Sutcliffe 2015, 78).

In healthcare, the patient and family customers have expertise that they bring to the situation. They know their values and life constraints. They know their goals and pain levels. They know much about their own worlds that providers do not know. Yes, the highly trained clinical team has expertise as well. It is a both/and, not an either/or.

> It is not that the patient is always right or that the clinician is always right. The best courses of action come from considering the expertise of all.

The customer is the center of the organizational universe in healthcare. The customer is why healthcare leaders lead. The customer is the heart of the journey.

Questions to Contemplate

1. Whom do I serve? Who are my customers?
2. How might I create more dialogue with my customers?
3. What expertise resides in my customers that I need to see and understand, and what can I do to be able to see it?
4. How might I help my organization leverage the voice of our customers?

Part 2: The Individual Journey

	Internal	External
Individual	Values, beliefs, priorities, and motivation of the individual.	Actions and behaviors of the individual
Collective	Values and beliefs of the collective	Actions and behaviors of the collective

Internal-Individual perspective

The upper-left quadrant interprets and focuses on one's personal internal values, beliefs, and hidden maps or mindsets. These mindsets form our internal operating system, akin to a computer's internal operating system. Wilber offers that personal exploratory work within this dimension is a form of *waking up*. Deep personal change comes from the process of recognizing the mindsets that trigger our behaviors.

External-Individual perspective

The upper-right quadrant interprets and focuses on the actions of the individual as seen by others. It is within this dimension that mindsets manifest themselves in behaviors visible to others, though not always to ourselves. This quadrant encourages us to seek feedback from others so that we become conscious of both our actions and our impact on others.

The top half of Ken Wilber's Integral Theory model focuses on individual development. The upper-left quadrant is the starting point for the individual leader's developmental journey. It requires deep self-awareness to uncover the mindsets that govern behavior, and to become self-aware requires the discipline of self-reflection. The practice of self-reflection is foundational to all topics covered within this book. The exploration of this top-left quadrant fosters clarity of personal purpose. Who I am? What do I value? For what do I stand?

The upper-right quadrant of the model also focuses on the individual; whereas the left quadrant is from the inside out, the right upper quadrant is from the outside in. This dimension provides critical insights into how the behavior of an individual influences others and affects systems and structure.

Working in both upper dimensions brings about new insights and developmental opportunities to leadership abilities. Once a leader is fully present with her or his inner reality, personal transformation is possible. This personal clarity can be translated into conscious choices about actions and behaviors as represented by the upper-right quadrant in Wilber's model.

"Part 2: The Individual Journey" takes the leader on a personal exploration from the internal to the external: from awareness of what is deep inside oneself to how one shows up for those they lead.

Without reflection, we go blindly on our way, creating more unintended consequences and failing to achieve anything useful.

–Margaret Wheatley (2005, 205)

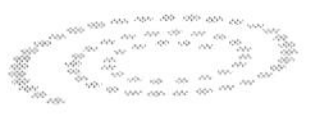

Develop Self Awareness

Self-awareness is essential to personal development and growth. It flows from the willing exploration of the vast unknown within each of us. Peter Senge, in his seminal work *The Fifth Discipline*, calls this discovery process *personal mastery:* the discipline of personal growth and learning (Senge 1990, 141). The discipline of self-awareness is the conscious pursuit of deep exploration into who we are as individuals, what is important to us (purpose), and where we want to go (vision). It is through the ongoing learning process about ourselves, both our gifts and shortcomings, that we can begin the personal change process essential to effectively leading both ourselves and others.

Self-Awareness. Conscious knowledge of one's own character, feelings, motives, and desires.

Self-awareness fuels positive change by growing an individual's understanding of the current reality and that of a desired future reality. The desire to close the gap between these two polarities causes a creative tension (Figure 2). This is the tension between where we are—our current reality—and where we want to be—our vision. This tension serves as a disruptive force creating a *dis-ease* with our current reality while energizing us into purposeful action to achieve the desired future state or vision.

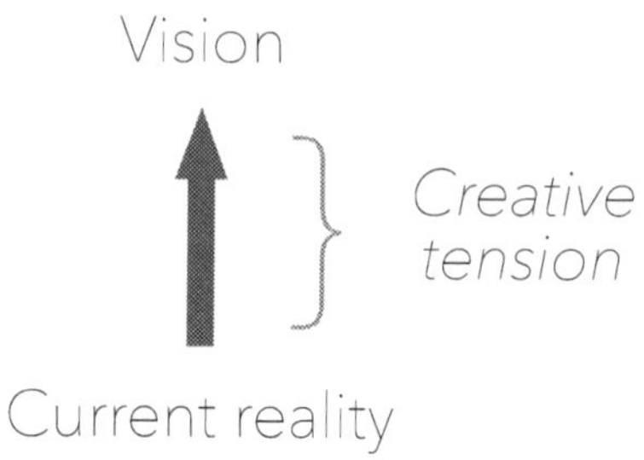

Figure 2: Tension is created when striving to achieve a new vision during the move from current to future state.

Navigating oneself and subsequently an organization through the creative tension of closing the gap between the current reality and the vision is a journey. The term *journey* implies that this is a continual process. It is seldom a smooth, straight line to the destination. It is akin to navigating across water with strong currents and eddies revealing unexpected challenges along the way. It is on this journey of personal and organizational growth, with the requisite challenges and conflicts, that rich, new insights and results are realized. To effectively navigate this journey requires conscious leadership. Hence, self-awareness is an essential leadership trait for leading oneself and an organization along the improvement journey.

The level of leaders' self-awareness has proven to be a strong predictor of overall personal and organizational effectiveness. Leaders who are self-aware are more successful in promoting individual learning and growth, as well as reaching individual and organizational goals. Leaders who are self-aware thoughtfully examine their own values, beliefs, and goals. In a sense, to be self-aware in this way is to come to a deep understanding of what might be called one's personal internal operating system. Such an operating system governs an individual's behavior much like a computer's operating system. A personal operating system translates the input from the external world and manifests itself through visible actions. It is only through this deep self-understanding that the leader can begin to create personal change while engaging associates toward improved organizational effectiveness. One must be honest with oneself about motivations, desires, and inclinations before creating a transforming environment for others.

Hence, the leadership challenge starts with self. To be effective, leaders need the will and courage to hold the tension between their individual current realities and their desired visions for their future selves. Strong self-awareness will enable a leader to hold and leverage the creative tension essential to make this transition from current to future state.

Developing the capacity for deep self-awareness happens most reliably when engaging in the practice of *self-reflection*. A bit of cross-cultural input can help illuminate the *what* and *how* of self-reflection. A central tenet of Japanese culture is **hansei**, a personal and group process of deep reflection to better understand failure and success. This philosophy of life drives leaders to take on the role of the student. The student learns through rigorous dialogue with and feedback from others as well as through individual internal contemplation.

> **Hansei:** The Japanese principle of reflection, characterized by owning one's mistakes and committing to improvement.

Self-reflection can occur in quiet solitude or in the midst of others. The key to reflective practices is being open to the honest voice either inside one's own head or to the voices of others who either observe or are recipients of one's leadership behaviors. While it is not likely any leader will ever achieve perfection, self-reflective practices allow leaders to learn from each experience and continually improve their leadership behaviors so that they are able to provide greater value to those they serve: their employees and—ultimately—their patients, families, and community.

Self-reflection and its reward of self-awareness cannot be thought of as passive exercises, new age meditation, or soft science. Self-reflection is hard and demanding interior work that fuels observable exterior change. As with most rehabilitation programs, self-refection begins with admitting that one had a problem, weakness, or blind spot. Self-reflection demands personal responsibility. It requires a willingness to ask deep questions and demand answers of oneself. It is initiated by the questions people ask themselves. For those not sure of how to begin this self-questioning path, the "Questions to Contemplate" throughout this book are a place to start.

> "Learning without reflection is a waste. Reflection without learning is dangerous."
>
> –Confucius

Granted, it is a challenging task for leaders to become more self-aware in the midst of the organizational whirlwind in which they work. By committing to the following three activities, a leader can become intentional in and committed to self-reflection and self-awareness in everyday organizational life.

1. Seek Feedback from Others

It may seem oxymoronic to suggest that one might look outside to become more self-aware. The reality is that all individuals have blind spots, some large and some small. Self-awareness can be kick-started through feedback from others. To stop and ask for the input and observations from others can be eye-opening. That is not to say that feedback from others must be taken in its entirety and as truth, but the outside view can trigger helpful personal reflection.

One structured method frequently used to gain individual feedback and promote leadership self-reflection is some form of leadership assessment. The best assessments use a 360-degree format that includes input from the next level up, peers, and direct reports. Feedback is particularly helpful when it is received from these multiple viewpoints. This broad input, if honestly given, can enable leaders to self-reflect, become more self-aware, and ultimately modify leadership behaviors to improve personal effectiveness and the performance of the organization.

Lessons from the Field

A nurse coached by one of the authors aspired to be a CNO. Shortly out of nursing school, she began to achieve her career goals, becoming in succession an assistant nurse manager, nurse manager, and then a nurse director overseeing four nursing units. At the time of the coaching engagement, she had changed organizations and roles but had not risen to a CNO position. She could not see what others could see. Her controlling style of leadership was not acceptable to prospective employers. After engaging in a robust 360-degree feedback process, she began to see herself as others did. The process of self-reflection and letting go of ineffective leadership habits was not easy, but she began to shift her leadership style. She internalized these new behaviors, was soon hired as a CNO in a mid-size healthcare facility, and became a highly respected leader in that organization.

2. Observe Oneself

Everyone has **mental models** that drive behaviors. Mental models play a major role in cognition, reasoning, and decision making. These are generally unspoken and over time become unconscious to the holder. Thus, an essential self-reflective practice to uncover mental models is to observe and reflect on one's own actions. To focus deliberately on personal actions and reactions, a leader can then ask questions such as those that follow: *Why did I say that? What was my motivation for doing that? What do I really want in this situation? If I could do that over, what would I do differently? How do I wish I could restructure my relationship with others?* Such questions help surface mental models and enable a leader to determine which are helpful and which are not. Ultimately, a leader can choose to maintain or challenge personal mental models and make conscious decisions about how to most effectively frame the world. The way we view the world drives how we interact with the world.

Mental Models: Thought processes or representations about how things work.

In essence, this is a practice of reflection on observations in order to rewire one's internal operating system. There are many supporting tools that can facilitate this work. Daily journaling of observations and reflections is one such practice. Another is feedback analysis as developed by Peter Drucker (Drucker 1999). In this simple technique, an individual documents expected outcomes from personal actions and decisions for a period of time and then compares the actual results with what was expected. Alignment and gaps uncovered through this method can create a rich feedback loop over time.

3. Be Aware of Others

> "Leadership is connected with the deepest parts of ourselves. It has much more to do with character, courage, and conviction than it does with specific skill or even competencies."
>
> -Robert Anderson & William Adams (2016, 29)

The pursuit of deeper self-awareness also entails being conscious of others: their words and behaviors that influence one's own actions. A leader who is curious and open-minded about the different types of people learns to identify the positive as well as negative behavior interactions that influence individual and group performance. Being aware of others creates a reciprocity in the relationship, which builds trust and respect. It is a form of deeply seeing others and not only hearing their words but also acknowledging how others are in that moment of interaction. It is a suspension of judgment, both of oneself and others, so one can attend to the full experience of the interaction. This acute awareness of others and oneself creates a continual learning feedback loop for the leader. It expands personal and group effectiveness. Paying attention enhances one's flexibility in actions.

The three forms of reflective practice described previously contribute to the essential inner personal work of the upper-left quadrant of Wilber's model. This individual development work supports defining personal purpose and gifts and surfaces fears and obstacles that may impede personal leadership growth. A leader who seriously pursues this path of self-awareness must do so with intellectual honesty and a sustained commitment of time and energy. This internal journey is the starting place for both personal development and organizational improvement. As we explore the "Lead with Purpose and Vision" and "Foster Humility" chapters in this book, it is evident that the practice of developing self-awareness is a fundamental practice for effective leaders.

The following questions are provided to help you initiate or continue your inner system exploration. Additional tools for self-reflection can be found in the "Self-Awareness Tools, Methods, and Approaches" section at the back of the book.

Questions to Contemplate

1. What do I value and believe?
2. How do my words and actions give life to my values and beliefs?
3. What self-reflective practices can I engage in to learn more about myself?
4. When was the last time I sought feedback from others regarding my actions and behaviors?

They all agree that leaders are made, not born, and made more by themselves than by any external means... they agree that no leader sets out to be a leader per se but rather to express him/herself freely and fully... Becoming a leader is synonymous with becoming yourself. It is precisely that simple, and it's also that difficult... First and foremost, find out what it is you're about and be that.

—Warren Bennis (2009, 396)

Lead With Purpose & Vision

An effective leader engages in an ongoing exploration of leadership **purpose** and **vision**. Without defined purpose and a clear vision, the leader sets forth on a rudderless journey toward an unknown destination.

> **Purpose** defines who you are. It reflects your passions and values. It provides clarity as you set goals. Your sense of purpose steers how you want your story to go.

Leadership purpose is the leader's sense of what is important, what and how to contribute to the greater good of the larger community, and how to serve others to achieve that greater good. It is a grounding that excites both one's head and heart. Without leadership purpose, a leader can find himself or herself adrift or tossed by the storms of the daily organizational whirlwind.

> **Vision**: An image of the desired future. Vision emerges from our imagination and sparks the creative process that propels us forward.

In comparison, **vision** is an image of the future state. It provides direction and sparks the creative powers needed to move forward. Vision propels leaders and provides courage to take risks, often beyond what is deemed possible. It provides leaders with the means to build relationships with others who share their vision, thereby creating a community. Vision, along with purpose, unites people in purposeful intent and action.

The deep practice of clarifying leadership purpose and vision brings forth in leaders not only their reason for leading but also a deeper understanding of their role within their organization and community. This introspective process animates leaders' creative powers and benefits both leaders and those they lead. By example and invitation, leaders shepherd not only their own personal growth but also the development of the organization as a whole and the individuals within it.

Without care and nurturing, purpose and vision can be destroyed by the difficult demands of everyday work life. Research of bedside nursing has shown that the current stressors of the caregiving process can have a detrimental effect on nurses' purpose. One nurse shared during a study of vocational calling, "There is a numbness of heart that diminishes my spirit and ability to care" (Kirkwood 2003, 171).

This phenomenon is not limited solely to care providers. It also affects employees at all levels, including senior leaders. The rigors

Lessons from the Field

The senior leaders at a health system have never lost sight of the mission of the sisters who started the hospital over a century ago: to inspire hope and contribute to health and well-being by providing the best care to every patient. Every day these leaders strive to maintain their own personal purpose connected to the organization's mission and enhance the shared sense of purpose of service to patients among providers and other team members. They do this by reminding everyone of the organization's spiritual roots and encouraging everyone to work together and support each other for the patients' benefit. In words and actions, these leaders exemplify the vision of caring and healing first promulgated by the sisters. Leaders emphasize building relationships with patients and their family members, and they work tirelessly to create an environment that emphasizes safe clinical practice and patient care.

of the daily routine in healthcare, the constant external stressors, and the bureaucratic processes in healthcare all contribute to the diminishment of a leader's purpose. The internal and external demands in healthcare can be all consuming, creating a diversion from personal and organizational purpose. To remain true to one's purpose amidst the challenges of a hectic personal and professional life, it is imperative that leaders regularly use self-reflective practices as discussed in the previous chapter. The very real act of pausing to reflect on one's individual purpose creates the ability to see possibilities or visions of a future that is better than today. Reconnecting to the original dream that brought a leader to his or her current state of leading can be an energizing activity. In addition to re-energizing a leader's head and heart, this reconnection brings a prioritizing power that allows leaders to jettison activities that add no value to vision or purpose. In our decades of working with healthcare leaders around the world, we have heard many speak of their *ah-ha moments* when they acknowledged that they had lost connection with their leadership calling. We have heard numerous

Lessons from the Field

One of the authors facilitated a leadership workshop designed to help leaders reconnect with personal purpose. A participant, the head of a large and successful nonprofit agency, clearly stated his purpose was to raise money. Throughout the two days, he held to this purpose. He resisted full participation in every activity. At the closing, he expressed frustration about the waste of his time. A month later in a follow-up session, he shared how wrong he had been about the workshop and himself. He had not realized how confused he was about his leadership purpose and vision. He acknowledged that he had lost his way in the relentless whirlwind of fundraising. With a touch of relief, he recounted how he rediscovered his true purpose through the workshop's reflective practices. His true purpose was not to raise money, though fundraising was important. It was to foster change in the community. He was passionate about that, and he recommitted to his role in leading that change effort.

effective leaders recount that flash of inspiration when they realized their levels of individual status were no longer sufficient for personal fulfillment and the success of the organization. It was in those moments that they reconnected to their higher leadership purpose. They accepted the need to change. Indeed, many discovered their current ways of leading were at times counter-productive to the desired results. It is in moments of self-reflection and realization that true shifts in mind and consciousness begin.

Finally, it is important to remember that the practice of discerning leadership purpose and envisioning the future is ongoing. It is not a *one and done* process. Individuals evolve, as does the environment. Purpose and vision must be revisited and tended to remain alive.

Lessons from the Field

Bob Anderson shares a powerful story of how he found his purpose early in his career. He used a series of reflective practices, including a must haves exercise (Anderson & Adams 2016, 240). In this exercise, he contemplated what his 6 to 12 must-haves in life were. Then, of the two or three that mattered most to him, he asked himself the following: Why do I care about these? What does it mean for my future? This self-reflective questioning opened both his deeper desire to serve and the creativity he innately possessed.

The internal work of remaining connected to purpose maintains a leader's true north. Then, with this clarity of purpose, the leader can mobilize his or her values and beliefs into positive actions to realize personal and organizational vision. Without this inner work at the individual level, the organizational shift will not happen. Hence, organizational change truly starts at the personal level. This is the *change within a change* that must begin within Wilber's internal–individual and external–individual quadrants. There is no organizational change without personal change. The whirlwind

Lessons from the Field

The newly hired CEO of a large academic medical center committed to rounds on every unit within his first two months on the job. During a visit to the Environmental Services Department, he asked one of the staff members to explain what she did in that department. She proudly replied that she helped save lives. Pleasantly surprised by this response, he asked her to elaborate. She told him that the work they do cleaning rooms and equipment was vital to patient safety and the effective functioning of the hospital. He left impressed by this staff member and the department as a whole, and he developed a desire to foster this same level of purpose in every provider, associate, and himself.

of the healthcare environment creates unparalleled distractions to leaders at all levels of the organization. This dissonance leads to reactive behaviors, as exemplified by rapidly shifting priorities and erratic behaviors. Clarity and focus on what is personally and organizationally essential helps anchor leaders and prevents anxiety-driven decision making. Ever deepening self-awareness promotes stability and intention in actions.

Questions to Contemplate

1. What is my leadership purpose and vision?
2. What are my six to eight must-haves to achieve my leadership purpose and vision?
3. Which of those are most important? Why are these most important to me?
4. How am I actively (and daily) contributing to achieving my personal vision and purpose?

The big *ah-ha* for me was when I realized that it was not helpful for me to have and provide the answer before anyone else. I was no longer valued as the answer man or the smartest guy in the room. It starts with the leader. We were not successful early on because we missed the shift in how we needed to lead. We were still operating from the paradigm that leaders needed to have the answers. It was a difficult change and one I am still working on after several years of practice.

–John Gizdic (2016)

Foster Humility

> **Humility**: The freedom from pride or arrogance. The quality or state of being humble.

The leadership attribute of **humility** is present and noticeable in leaders who have successfully led organizational improvement journeys. Humility is modesty and restraint without the destructive effects of out-sized ego or hubris. Humility is courageous. It is the willingness to admit mistakes and seek out guidance. Humility is self-respect without excessive self-promotion.

Humble leaders let go of two common tendencies: the need to be seen as competent in all things and the need to be seen as infallible. Leaders who feel these needs are often haunted by the fear of being found incompetent. This is referred to as the *imposter phenomenon*, as coined by Susan Imes and Pauline Rose Clance (Weir 2013). Imes and Clance became aware of this phenomenon when counseling students at a liberal arts college. The students felt their success was a fluke despite their good test scores and recommendations.

Hugh Kearns deepened the exploration of this condition in *The Imposter Syndrome* (Kearns 2015). Kearns differentiated between *imposter feelings* and the *imposter syndrome*. Those with imposter feelings occasionally feel that they are not up to the tasks before them, despite evidence to the contrary. Such sporadic feelings usually pass. Almost 70% of people have the occasional feeling of being an imposter. Individuals with imposter syndrome, on the other hand, feel like frauds a great deal of the time, despite clear evidence that they are not. These feelings affect what the individuals think, feel, and do. Howard Schultz, the former CEO of Starbucks, admitted that he and many executives have experienced this fear. "Very few people, whether you've been in that job before or not, get into the seat and believe today that they are now qualified to be the CEO. They're not going to tell you that, but it's true" (Molinsky 2016).

> "As a shame researcher, I know the very best thing to do in the midst of a shame attack is totally counterintuitive: Practice courage and reach out!"
>
> - Brené Brown (2000, 9)

In many healthcare organizations, leaders are promoted on the basis of their effectiveness in previous positions where they relied on technical expertise. As leaders rise in the organization, they move away from that core expertise and can increasingly feel alone. Their decisions and actions are subject to review by everyone else in the organization. This sense of ongoing critical judgment can amplify the fear of being discovered to be unworthy, and the individuals feel shame. This fear and sense of shame causes leaders to struggle mightily to appear wise, knowledgeable, and ultimately correct in all opinions and decisions. The effort to be perfect and all-knowing is irrational but powerful.

The further leaders travel from their core expertise, the deeper this fear and shame can become. The situation can be exacerbated by a leader with a dominant ego, creating toxicity for both the leader and those he or she leads. Problems brought to the leader are often complex and may not be in the leader's specific area of expertise. The answers are not intuitive, and solving them can require new learning. The fact is that most organizational problems are too great for one person to completely understand and effectively solve. However, leaders try to put on a brave face and go it alone, pronouncing solutions and unilateral decisions on demand as asked.

Put another way, the underlying assumption for many leaders is that if they acknowledge not knowing something, they are not doing the job they were selected to do. Paradoxically, when a leader is willing to acknowledge he or she doesn't know everything, trusts the problem-solving process, and involves others to learn together, the leader's knowledge and skills grow. In addition, this approach grows the skills of the others also engaged in the dialogue. When a leader is humble and tamps down the emotions of fear and pride, great things can be accomplished by the leader and his or her team. Healthcare leaders who are honest when they do not know something actually gain the respect of those with whom they work. It is this act of being humble that engenders trust and respect from other team members.

> Do you know how you can tell someone is truly humble? I believe there is one simple test: because they consistently observe and listen, the humble improve. They don't assume, "I know the way." ...Humility engenders learning because it beats back the arrogance that puts blinders on. It leaves you open for the truths to reveal themselves, so you don't stand in your own way.
>
> –Wynton Marsalis (2005, 11)

Successful leadership, then, requires an internal shift from ego to humility. This shift has been recognized and reinforced by a number of thought leaders and theorists. The versions of this move have been variously described as follows:

- Serve first, then lead (Greenleaf 1977).
- Ask first, then tell only if necessary (Schein 2013).
- Seek first to understand then to be understood (Covey 2004).
- Defer to the expertise of others (Weick & Sutcliffe 2015).

> "I frequently remind myself to trust the problem-solving process and the expertise of those who truly know the work to get great solutions to both simple and complex problems."
>
> –Kathy Wilde (2016)

Each of these expressions of leadership clearly shows that the self-aware and humble leader is willing to subordinate personal ego to learn from, trust, and be in a relationship with others. This shift to leading with humility requires *letting go*. The leader must let go of his or her ego. Both the leader and the followers must let go of the image of the leader as the go-to person with all the correct answers. This can be a difficult challenge for both a leader and her or his followers as the belief that someone—anyone—can always know what is right is comforting. But for individual and organizational growth, the myth of the all-powerful, wise superhero must be abandoned. When a leader loosens a tight grip on the image of infallibility once felt as a source of power, that leader regains sight of purpose. To lead in this transformative way means that one's actions are always guided by values and beliefs.

Lessons from the Field

An executive of a large academic medical system stopped by a newly constructed, inner-city outpatient clinic built to serve the poorest and most needy residents. She arrived 45 minutes before the clinic opened to meet with providers and personnel. When she arrived, she observed a large number of people waiting to gain entrance to the facility. Curious as to why so many people were outside waiting and resisting the urge to make assumptions, she spoke with them and discovered that the city's bus schedules forced many people to arrive early. After speaking with physicians, staff members, and facility leaders, they collectively agreed to change the clinic's hours of operation so the facility would open earlier to accommodate its customers. The humility to ask and learn created positive change for all.

There is a constancy of purpose that comes from a deep level of self-awareness and clarity of purpose.

Letting go of ego and the façade of infallibility requires conscious attention. It requires self-awareness that grows out of self-reflective practices. As discussed in the "Develop Self Awareness" chapter, this learning about hard-wired habits, internal operating systems, true gifts, and weaknesses comes only with difficult inner work.

It is within the individual–internal quadrant of Wilber's model that this letting go of ego and embracing humility emerges and gives rise to the individual–external behaviors of effective leadership. This internal work, which leads to external action, demonstrates Wilber's concept of personal development as both a *waking up* and a *growing up* (Wilber 2016, 10). The contemplative questions that follow are intended to initiate both the uncovering as well as letting go of these unhelpful mindsets.

Questions to Contemplate

1. When and how often do I feel the need to be right and to have all the answers?

2. When do I fail to ask before I tell?

3. Why do I lead with telling rather than asking?

4. What would happen if I were to consistently lead by asking and serving?

Real learning gets to the heart of what it means to be human. Through learning we re-create ourselves. Through learning we become able to do something we never were able to do. Through learning we perceive the world and our relationship to it. Through learning we extend our capacity to create, to be part of the generative process of life. There is within each of us a deep hunger for this type of learning.

—Peter Senge (1990, 14)

Become a Voracious Learner

> "The greatest obstacle to discovering new things is not ignorance but the illusion of knowledge."
>
> –W. Terry Howell (2016)

Great leaders not only take responsibility for their own learning by showing humility and admitting they do not know everything but also by working to actively increase their knowledge. That is, they adopt a student mindset and become voracious learners.

Two of the most well-known figures from the Renaissance period, Michelangelo and Leonardo Da Vinci, illustrate the power of the student mindset. Both men were visionaries, painters, architects, and engineers who changed the course of art and technology. Both were lifelong learners, constantly pushing themselves to improve and do better. Both are credited with frequently saying "*Ancora imparo*," a Latin phrase that means, "I am still learning." It is said that Michelangelo wrote this inscription on a sketch he drew at the age of 87 (Training for Warriors 2011).

By establishing a rigorous personal learning process, effective leaders model the importance and benefits of individual growth. In addition, these leaders demonstrate how individual learning is tied to organizational success. Such leaders create a contagious spirit of curiosity that infects those around them.

The initial step in developing a student mindset is to be purposeful and humble in adopting the role of a student. Purposeful adoption requires clarity of personal vision and honesty in one's assessment of gaps in knowledge or skills. When one consciously adopts a

Lessons from the Field

A chief information officer used his military background to solve most problems he encountered. As his career advanced in healthcare, he noted that the problems were increasingly complex and he did not always have all the answers. He also received feedback from supervisors, peers, and his direct reports that his habit of telling others what to do was deflating to his team. He decided to learn how he could show up differently as a leader. To identify what new habits he could incorporate, he read a variety of materials, networked with others in professional organizations, and actively sought out others who could coach him. After study and reflection, he chose to experiment with letting go of having all the answers and began to inquire and learn from his direct reports. While not as easy as giving orders, this leader observed that when he asked questions and solicited ideas from his reports, their skills in problem solving became stronger and frequently resulted in more effective solutions. As a byproduct, his team's engagement increased greatly.

student mindset, it is an acknowledgement that personal improvement is ongoing and never-ending. This intention to keep learning creates the discipline to persevere despite the ongoing and seductive intrusions of pop-up problems and noise within the organization. It requires just such discipline to maintain a student mindset when regulators arrive unannounced, patient complaints must be addressed, IT systems go down, or reimbursement rules change. Such emergent events can draw leaders into a purely reactive mode. Loud voices calling, "Fire!" can drown out the call to learning. The turbulent healthcare environment necessitates that effective leaders incorporate space for learning and balance the time they spend in reactive responses versus proactive personal learning and growth.

Learning can take place quickly when integrated into the daily activities of a leader, adding a positive energy to the workplace and inspiring continual development of the leader's effectiveness.

Learning can occur through varying kinds of activities. Five approaches that strongly promote a student mindset and encourage learning are outlined in the following sections.

1. Observe the Work

> "Knowledge has to be improved, challenged, and increased constantly, or it vanishes."
>
> -Anon

Going to where a problem occurs and observing firsthand is a powerful method for learning. This is known as *going to the gemba*. *Gemba* is a Japanese term meaning *the real place* and is used to denote the site where work is done. Observing real work and its associated problems is a far more effective method for achieving real learning than reading or listening to an account of the work. Observing for real learning requires a disciplined process to see first without judgment. One must begin by watching without comment or intervention. A structured process for observation using a template allows leaders to focus on learning the process instead of jumping to solutions. Often, observation is followed with the next activity of inquiry and analysis.

Lessons from the Field

A group of executives spent time observing the work at the frontline prior to the replacement of the clinical and business information systems. During one such session, the CEO observed outpatient registration. While completing their tasks, staff members got up frequently from their desks to pick up papers from a common printer. When the CEO shared this observation with the staff and asked why the work required so much motion, he learned that the staff had requested that an additional printer be bought and placed close to the registration desk. Staff then informed the CEO that the request had been denied during executive meetings. Observation created new learning and provided insight that was not present at the time decisions were made about allocating funds.

2. Inquire Inside the Organization

To fuel even more learning from inside the organization, observation can be coupled with inquiry and analysis. Leaders who ask thoughtful questions can deepen their understanding of situations. By asking open and non-blaming questions of those who have a greater knowledge of a process or problem, the leader demonstrates respect for those team members. Asking thoughtful questions helps the leader and the process experts determine the root causes of problems before solutions are selected and implemented.

3. Learn from Outside the Organization

Another step in adopting a student mindset is to learn from outside of the organization—even from outside of healthcare. Great leaders are known to be voracious readers on subjects within their own industry as well as other industries. Similarly, attending workshops and conferences can broaden a leader's viewpoint and allow him or her to imagine new possibilities. Site visits to organizations

Lessons from the Field

The medical staff of a large health system had heard their administrator advocate for a team-based care model in support of population health initiatives. In theory, the physicians endorsed the concepts, but they were not ready to fully support the personal changes necessary. Some of the physician leaders invited physicians and administrators from another organization to share their history of implementing team-based care. These presenters shared their implementation journey and the benefits experienced by the patients, staff, and providers. The local medical staff members were enlightened by what they heard and became advocates for change in their own practices. They drove implementation of daily huddles, care coordination structures, and activities to identify patient outliers who were missing preventative screenings. One year later, after metrics for prevention activities significantly improved, physicians who previously were the greatest resistors were now the most vocal champions for the change.

inside and outside of healthcare can also be thought provoking. Though every organization is different and it is unwise to try to install another organization's solution without adaptation, learning what others have tried sparks innovation.

4. Experiment

The first three approaches listed here generate fuel for learning. That fuel, when fed into the engine of experimentation, can be converted into both personal and organizational learning. The scientific method can be used to test ideas and move from hypotheses to evidence, learning what works or does not work in particular situations.

5. Engage in Coaching Relationships

Everyone has blind spots regarding personal and organizational performance. Coaching can help illuminate these blind spots. Many continuously growing leaders work with respectful and honest coaches who are willing to tell them the truth. Some healthcare organizations have internal staff who serve as leader coaches and help explore leaders' personal and organizational improvement opportunities. In some cases, a direct supervisor may be able to provide valuable coaching advice. If these internal resources are not available, leaders may need to look outside of the organization to find a coach who is objective. Also, just as leaders need coaching, they must develop coaching skills so they can provide input to others. For example, leaders may find opportunities to act as a coach to someone who reports to them.

It should also be noted that coaching can be a reciprocal activity. Those we coach often have something to teach us as well. They can provide honest feedback and be a catalyst for our own reflection on how we have shown up as coaches and leaders.

W. Edwards Deming was a fervent student and committed teacher. In his 14 Points, he challenged everyone to *institute a vigorous program of education and self-improvement.* Actively engaging in the approaches listed in this chapter can help leaders maintain a student mindset and engage in continuous and voracious learning. Through the practices and Questions to Contemplate within this chapter and the previous three chapters, leaders may be intentionally rewiring their internal operating systems as they explore the internal and external individual dimensions of Wilber's integral model. This chapter, along with the next chapter on systems thinking, will help with continuing to gain awareness of our personal beliefs and values and translate these into collective actions, which are further explored in Part 3.

Questions to Contemplate

1. When did I assume the role of learner today?
2. What did I learn about myself and about my organization today?
3. When and how have I resisted learning?
4. What can I do to encourage everyone in my organization to become a voracious learner?

The obligation of any component is to contribute its best to the system, not to maximize its own production, profit, or sales, nor any other competitive measure.

A good example of a system, well optimized, is a good orchestra.

—W. Edwards Deming (1993, 99)

Cultivate Systems Thinking

"Do your best."

"Achieve your goals."

"Win!"

All of these admonitions to excel appear to be worthy instructions. Why would anyone *not* want to do her best, achieve his goals, or win? What might give a person pause before he or she drives, drives, drives toward individual targets?

System: A set of components that are interdependent and work in concert to accomplish a common aim.

The cause for pause in this drive toward achieving higher levels of individual performance is **systems** thinking. Because healthcare leaders are part of an organization, they have more to consider than just their own individual aims. To be effective leaders, they must always think both broadly and deeply about problems, issues, concerns, and goals.

Think Broadly

To think broadly is to see one's place in a larger context—to see one's role as a component of a larger whole. It is to look left and right, front and back, to see the context within which one is situated. For example, the leader who thinks broadly looks beyond the local business unit and sees connections and interdependencies throughout the organization. This broad-thinking individual knows that for the healthcare system to work well, units and departments must engage, support, and serve each other. No function can be an island unto itself.

In contrast, when one's focus is narrow and a leader views the world only from his or her own perspective, it is easy to see success as a local endeavor. If a leader has individual business objectives, particularly if they are tied to appraisal rankings and pay for performance, *success* can be viewed as achieving those objectives without regard to any broader context. And if one leader's win ultimately means his or her colleagues lose, then the system overall suffers.

This is the phenomenon that W. Edwards Deming referred to as **sub-optimizing** the system by optimizing the parts (Deming 1990). His frequently used example of this was a car engine. If the very best, or optimized, parts of every kind of auto engine are found and put together, the result is an engine that does not run. That is because these superior parts are not designed to work together.

> **Sub-Optimization**: Efforts to improve or optimize the performance of a component of a system to the detriment of the total system, perhaps even to the defeat of the system goals.

The following example illustrates this in a healthcare organization and returns to the prior business example. Imagine that an inpatient orthopedic unit leader is held to very strict goals regarding labor costs, including overtime. This leader's individual performance rating, as well as bonus and pay raise, are tied to meeting these goals. Further imagine that this unit is not particularly stressed with high census at this moment. At the same time, the med-surg inpatient unit needs temporary staff for a critical, urgent, and unanticipated peak volume. If loaning staff will negatively affect the orthopedic unit's labor budget, at the very least this leader will think long and hard before lending resources. This leader may decide to offer those resources if a charge-back to the other department can be arranged, or the unit leader may withhold some or all of the requested resources if not. This seems a rational response to the system that is in place, but it is a response that can negatively affect the organization overall. If it is best for the organization to use any and all needed resources to deal with problems, denying or delaying those resources can waste time and compromise organizational performance. The orthopedic unit leader may be able to preserve the local labor budget but at a cost to the organization as a whole.

The leader in this case is guided by the incentive structure the organization has put in place. Any message of working as a team or thinking as a system is degraded if, at the same time, the organization puts in place systems and incentives that reward and recognize independent or singular action. Leaders who think in terms of systems not only take action with a broadened view of how those actions affect the greater organization but also push back on structural components of the organization that incent or incline toward optimization of the parts—and hence the sub-optimization of the whole.

Think Deeply

Every organization has problems to be solved. Some organizations value and perpetuate the myth of the hero leader who wanders the organization with a fire extinguisher, finding flames and putting them out. Indeed, when there is a fire, it is important to put it out. But the hero leader image is a very limited view of leadership. Effective leaders must look deeper than the presenting fire. If the observable problem is the tip of an iceberg, 90% of it sits below the surface (see Figure 3).

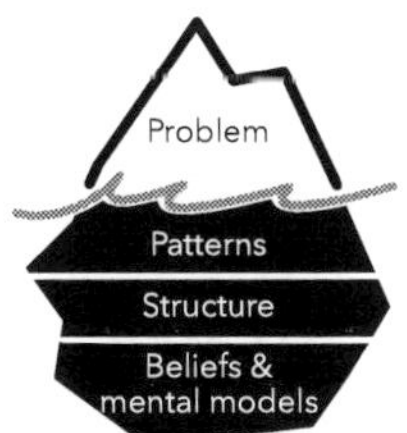

Figure 3: A problem iceberg shows only 10% at the surface, while 90% of the problem remains below.

Lessons from the Field

A group of cardiothoracic surgeons were upset because an undue number of cases were being delayed or cancelled. This disrupted an already tight schedule and upset patients and their families as well as the surgeons. No one was sure what was causing the problem. Upon examination, there were issues before and after surgery. The pre-admission process varied by surgeon and was convoluted. This led to missing critical items that were not discovered until the patient was being prepped. Those cases had to be rescheduled. In addition, patients were not stepped down from the Cardiac Care Unit (CCU) to the Progressive Care Unit in a timely manner. This caused CCU beds to be tied up as morning cases were completed, which forced those patients to be held in the OR and delayed the start of subsequent cases.

Efforts were dedicated to creating a more consistent and rational pre-admission testing program and a more timely and evidence-based patient step down. Systems thinking and these improvements eliminated many pre-surgery issues and freed up post-surgical beds.

When leaders function at the visible problem level, they work on the individual event, dealing only with the immediate and observable. That is required, but it is not enough.

Below the surface is the root cause system: the patterns, structure, and beliefs and mental models that contribute to and allow the problem to occur. In healthcare, team members are acclimated to this concept. They are, by regulation, required to conduct root cause analyses on significant negative or sentinel events. The idea behind this requirement is that by digging under the individual event, the team can determine the cause that could recur and trigger similar problems in the future. This digging must go deep to achieve true systems thinking.

Lessons from the Field

The surgeons at a hospital wanted a new piece of equipment. Given the large expense, they collected much data and prepared a thorough return on investment analysis to convince the executive team to make the purchase. In discussing the potential purchase, the surgeons learned that the executive team was just as concerned with the upstream and downstream impact on and capacity of other areas, such as pre-admission testing, recovery, and the step-down units. The surgery team was asked to talk with the other impacted areas and return to the executive team with plans for how those areas could accommodate the impact of the new technology.

What is often lacking is the transfer of this root cause thinking beyond catastrophic events to everyday problems. To think systemically, one must repeatedly and daily dig beneath problems, big and small, and think deeply about the underlying patterns and structures. It is also at this point that leaders begin to realize how distant in time the effects of actions can be. The effects of what one does today are often delayed beyond what is visible today.

By understanding the relational and time-dispersed nature of cause and effect, leaders begin to better understand the structure beneath events. This can be thought of as the scaffolding or dynamics that create the patterns that lead to events.

At the bottom of the iceberg is the belief system or mental model operating as the foundation and driver for everything above it. It is often in the dark, unarticulated, and unexamined. Organizational theorist Edgar Schein calls this level the realm of *basic assumptions*. These assumptions are taken for granted. They are the unspoken operating rules within a group. For example, some organizations build systems and operate with the belief that all people come to work wanting to do a good job, while others operate with the mental model that most people will try to get away with as much as possible. Schein states, "Basic assumptions … tend to be nonconfrontable and nondebatable, and hence are extremely difficult

> "It is only with the heart that one can see rightly; what is essential is invisible to the eye."
>
> -Antoine de Saint-Exupéry (1990, 63)

to change" (Schein 2010, 28). But leaders must change these basic assumptions if they want to create lasting positive improvement in the organization.

Robert Kegan and Lisa Laskow Lahey provide a compelling case for how to use an understanding of what lies below the surface to catalyze change. It is their assertion that understanding the deepest part of the iceberg and addressing it directly is the most powerful agent for transformation. They call this foundational origin of structure, patterns, and events "big assumptions." In the words of Kegan and Lahey, "Assumptions-taken-as-truth are what we mean by big assumptions. They are not so much the assumptions we have as they are the assumptions *that have us*" (Kegan & Lahey 2001, 68).

By identifying these assumptions—the unspoken, unquestioned, and unexamined source of an organization's equilibrium—a leader can act in an intentional way. He or she may articulate and address directly that underlying belief system to bring about true change.

The Inside Out of Systems Thinking

Thinking both broadly and deeply are necessary but not sufficient to thinking and acting systemically. The systems thinker must also consider the effect and place he or she has **in** a system while working **on** a system.

When working to improve the system, a leader is confronted with a paradox. To effectively see the system, the leader needs to take an outside view. The leader diagnoses the system from outside and applies change treatments from outside of the system to the system itself. However, leaders who are systems thinkers recognize that they are a part of the whole. Leaders cannot observe and act on a system without being or becoming part of that system. Therefore, leaders' own actions, patterns, structures, and beliefs or big assumptions must be part of the equation and open to examination. Leaders must recognize that their actions have import and impact on the system. A leader is a part of—not apart from—the system.

Hence, we have returned once again to self-awareness as a key to leadership effectiveness. In this case, it is the leader's self-awareness regarding his or her role in the system that supports the leader as a deep systems thinker. To use the language of Wilber, systems thinking requires the intersection of the individual and the collective and demands the connection of the internal and external. Systems thinking is an outside-in and inside-out activity.

It is also important to remember that systems thinking is not an end in itself. Systems thinking is intended to result in positive change, both personal and organizational. Indeed, there is no organizational change without personal change.

In systems thinking, there is a duality of the outside-in and inside-out approach as articulated in Wilber's model. This multi-dimensional process calls upon leaders to deeply challenge their thinking and behaviors from a broader systems awareness perspective and implement solutions without sub-optimizing the overall system. Systems thinking requires exploring three of the four quadrants within Wilber's model. Leaders may seek to see the patterns and structures that underlie the current system (collective–external), the patterns of personal behaviors (individual–external), and their own drivers of behavior (individual–internal). Ultimately, through this work, leaders influence the fourth quadrant, collective-internal, where organizational culture resides.

Questions to Contemplate

1. Where do I and my organization tend to optimize parts rather than the whole?

2. In what ways do I personally discourage systems thinking?

3. What can I do to use and encourage more systems thinking?
4. How can I better balance seeing the system from an outside view while recognizing my role in the system?

Part 3: The Organizational Journey

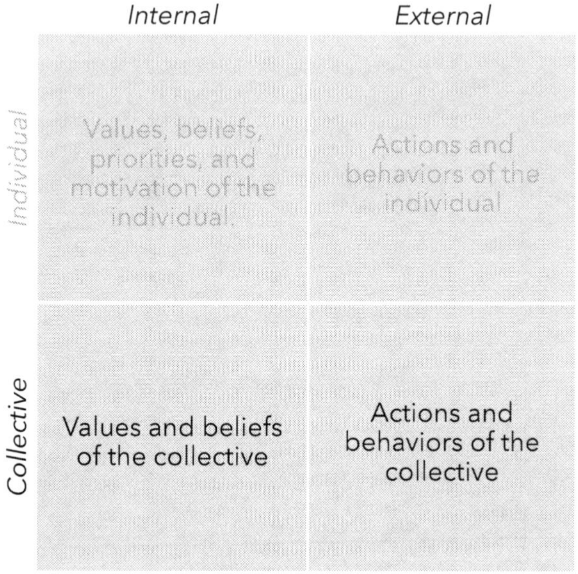

	Internal	*External*
Individual	Values, beliefs, priorities, and motivation of the individual.	Actions and behaviors of the individual
Collective	Values and beliefs of the collective	Actions and behaviors of the collective

Internal-Collective perspective

The lower-left quadrant is where the interior of the group is defined. Within this dimension reside the group's values, norms, shared habits, and purpose. In other words, this is where organizational culture exists. Culture is the internal operating system for the group and larger organization. This powerful and self-sustaining system is evidenced through the outward behaviors or artifacts of the group yet, like the individual operating system noted above, it is not visible through casual observation. It is with deliberate awareness and work within the other three quadrants that the culture can be understood and shaped.

External-Collective perspective

The lower-right quadrant is the dimension where the exterior of the organization is defined. The exterior is visible in the systems, structures, workflow design, and workplace practices. This is the province of most organizational change initiatives as leaders seek influence and control over these business elements.

The lower half of Wilber's Integral Theory model focuses on the collective nature of an organization. The lower-left quadrant contains the group or organization's internal operating system. It is this system of unwritten rules that we call *culture*. Like the deep exploration required to understand an individual operating system, one must be deliberate in seeking to decode the organization's operating system or culture.

The lower-right quadrant contains the organization's systems and structures. This is the dimension most often discussed and debated in organizations as it is readily visible. This high visibility can lull leaders into a false sense of surety regarding change initiatives. The common misconception is that if it can be seen it can be easily changed, but that is not true. This short-sighted view overlooks the system-ness of the visible parts and the underlying cultural dimensions that work to neutralize change initiatives and return the organization to status quo.

The focus of Part 3 builds upon the foundation laid in Part 2. It is the progression through the lower-right quadrant (collective–external) into the lower-left quadrant (collective–internal), which ultimately forms and influences the culture of the organization. Again, within each quadrant, there is a multitude of development opportunities. Yet without a systematic approach integrating these developmental opportunities from each, the results will be less than optimal and more than likely unsustainable.

The ability to execute strategy can be more important than the strategy itself.

–Robert Kaplan and David Norton (2001, 1)

Align Everyone with the Organization's Strategy

> **Strategy Deployment**: A process to align an organization's strategy with day-to-day functions and improvement activities.

Departments and business units within organizations often operate at cross purposes. Leaders sometimes unintentionally set this kind of behavior in motion and reinforce it through formal and informal reward systems as discussed previously in "Cultivate Systems Thinking." Sadly, yet predictably, the result is the optimization of one department or unit at the expense of others, resulting in frustrated staff members and poor overall service to patients and other customers. To overcome this fragmentation, one of the most important things a leader can do is to work daily to connect all parts of the organization to the organization's vision and strategy. It is imperative that leaders align everyone toward a common purpose and ensure all are working together to most effectively serve customers.

Organization-wide connectivity is enabled by what is known as **strategy deployment**. Based on the guiding principles of inclusion and respect, strategy deployment helps leaders drill down to the daily activities that everyone, from senior leaders to frontline staff, must accomplish to improve operational performance and achieve the organization's vision. To be effective at strategy deployment requires leaders to bring their best selves to the effort: to be humble; to acknowledge that they do not know everything; to adopt a systems approach; and to embrace the role of teacher, student, and coach.

Effective strategy deployment requires thoughtful planning, highly organized deployment, and ongoing review of the progress toward the plan. These three components might be thought of as the planning system depicted in Figure 4.

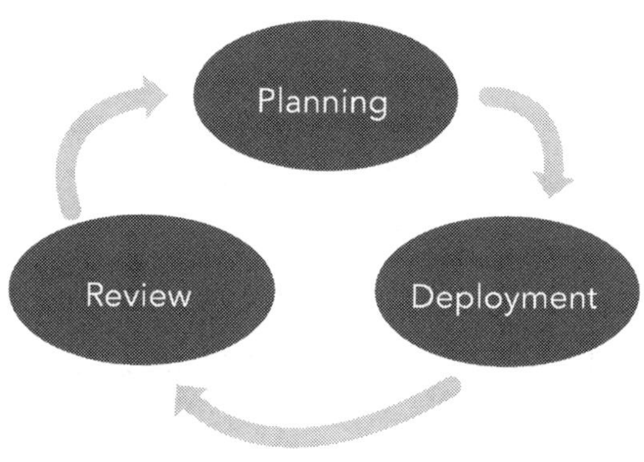

Figure 4: The components of a comprehensive system for deploying strategy throughout an organization.

A full exploration of strategic planning is beyond the scope of this book and worthy of its own treatise. However, it is helpful to consider a few tips that, when executed during the planning process, can translate into productive plan deployment.

Tips on Creating the Strategic Plan

Strategic planning is the process of deciding or confirming which community needs a healthcare organization will seek to meet and how it will improve to best meet those needs. Robust strategic plans articulate where the organization is headed, the actions needed to reach that destination, and the specific metrics by which progress and success will be evaluated. The following six actions contribute to a strategic plan that can be successfully deployed.

1. Look Three to Five Years Out

Successful organizations maintain a focus on the future by developing a three- to five-year strategic plan. By looking out several years, the organization can maintain a longer-term vision while working on items that are critical today. This constancy of purpose also allows strategic initiatives to come to full fruition as many of these projects take more than one year to complete. Even in a volatile industry such as healthcare, taking this longer view aids in focus. With this multi-year view, when environmental disruptions occur, the organization can thoughtfully maintain a steady course or consciously decide to change course.

2. Prioritize and Limit the Number of Strategic Goals

Vilfredo Pareto (1848–1923) was an engineer, sociologist, economist, political scientist, and philosopher. He is best known for his study of income distribution in Italy. Pareto found that approximately 80% of the land in Italy was owned by 20% of the population. He hypothesized that this 80/20 rule could be found in many situations, where 80% of an outcome is attributable to 20% of the causal variables. This 80/20 thinking came to be known as the Pareto Principle. It is not a law of nature and is not seen in every data set, but Pareto thinking is a broadly applicable and useful concept. It is particularly helpful in strategic planning.

> "The essence of strategy is choosing what not to do."
>
> -Michael Porter (1996, 70)

As a wise leader once stated, "If everything is important, then nothing is important." Given the finite resources and energy available to contemporary healthcare organizations, leaders must focus on a small number of goals, increasing the likelihood of successful progress. For a strategic plan to effectively drive progress and improvement, strategies must be limited to those few that will provide the highest return. Leaders need to focus everyone on the highest-leverage opportunities. In other words, of all that could be

> "There is nothing so useless as doing efficiently that which should not be done at all."
>
> -Peter F. Drucker (1963)

pursued, determine the 20% that will give the largest return on investment.

No exact prescribed number of strategies is perfect for all organizations, but four to eight is a reasonable range. To get to this concentrated small set of strategies, leaders must constantly return to Pareto thinking and combat the false sense of achievement that comes from having a long list of planned goals.

3. Ensure Balance in the Goals

Organizations can become narrowly focused on the loudest voices and emergent crises. In healthcare, these consuming demands are often in the regulatory environment where new quality requirements are born and in the financial arena as new reimbursement rules are generated. This limited view of what is important sometimes transfers into a strategic plan that is narrow and unbalanced. It behooves healthcare leaders to check their strategic goals for balance across dimensions of performance. Balance in strategic goals ensures that the organization is moving forward across multiple dimensions of performance and not just one. It also makes it more likely that every part of the organization will be touched by and engaged in pulling toward a balanced set of goals.

Some organizations use a set of four to six company-specific strategic pillars to balance the plan. These pillars often include categories such as quality, finance, patient experience, people development, and growth. Absent organizational pillars, a healthcare business might use a generic model of dimensions of performance for balance. Such a generic model is depicted as a diamond in Figure 5.

Figure 5: Dimensions of performance to achieve balance in deploying strategy in an organization.

Part of the power of this balanced view is that it helps avoid the trap of trade-off thinking. Trade-off thinking is the belief that improvement on one dimension of performance necessarily degrades another dimension. In fact, that is not true. With a balance and coordinated approach, strategy deployment and its related improvement work can simultaneously grow all dimensions of performance.

4. Set Evolutionary and Revolutionary Goals

Evolutionary goals are achieved through incremental, continuous improvement. Examples of such evolutionary goals include reducing length of stay, reducing the 30-day readmission rate, eliminating hospital-acquired infections, or improving operating margins. Revolutionary goals are breakthrough ideas with dramatic scope that move organizations into greater innovation and creativity. To establish alternative models of care via new technologies, develop strategic partnerships that expand scale and increase market presence, or fundamentally shift service offerings to improve healthy behaviors of our chronic disease patients would be revolutionary. Both evolutionary and revolutionary goals are necessary for or-

Alignment: In arrangement in a straight line or in correct or appropriate relative positions.

ganizations and should be incorporated into the three- to five-year strategic plan.

5. Designate an Executive Owner for Each Strategic Goal

It is critical to identify a single executive to take point on each strategic goal and to be accountable for seeing the assigned goal through to conclusion. The importance of naming only one individual to this role for each goal is that there can be no confusion over who leads the effort. There is a single point of accountability. The executive owner shepherds the deployment of strategic goals through analysis and catchball, which will be described later in this chapter. The executive owner also provides support horizontally across the organization, removing roadblocks and smoothing the path to progress.

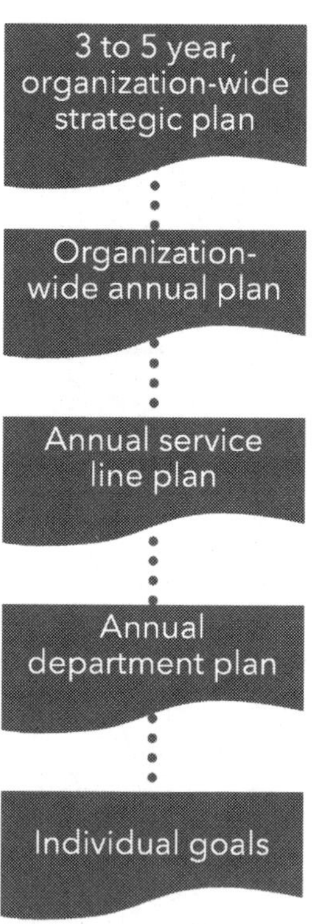

Figure 6. Strategy deployment fosters alignment between all activities, from individual behaviors to organizational strategy.

6. Translate the Three- to Five-Year Plan into an Annual Plan

Based on the organization's longer-term strategic direction and goals, leaders must next identify the short-term means for reaching these goals in the shorter term. An annual plan is essential. It guides the immediate tactical initiatives and activities needed to move the organization toward its strategic goals. Once the annual plan is drafted, deployment throughout the organization can begin.

Strategy Deployment

The power of strategy deployment lies in cascading goals throughout the organization so everyone knows how they contribute to important organizational priorities. With the caveat that healthcare businesses are organized in different ways and use differing language for their particular business units, Figure 6 is an example of the **alignment** that leaders should seek—from the broadest vision and strategy to individual behaviors through which patients and other customers are served.

To create these cascaded goals and logically linked plans requires much communication and coordination. This is best accomplished through a process known as *catchball.*

Catchball

Like the child's game where a ball is tossed from one person to another, catchball is a back-and-forth exchange between successive levels in the organization to ensure that the strategic goals are well understood and that there is strong alignment between strategy and initiatives undertaken across the organization. Figure 7 illustrates where catchball is typically done to flesh out plans and create alignment.

> **Catchball**: A two-way exchange between different levels in the organization to develop plans that translate strategic goals into initiatives that cascade down through the organization to the frontline.

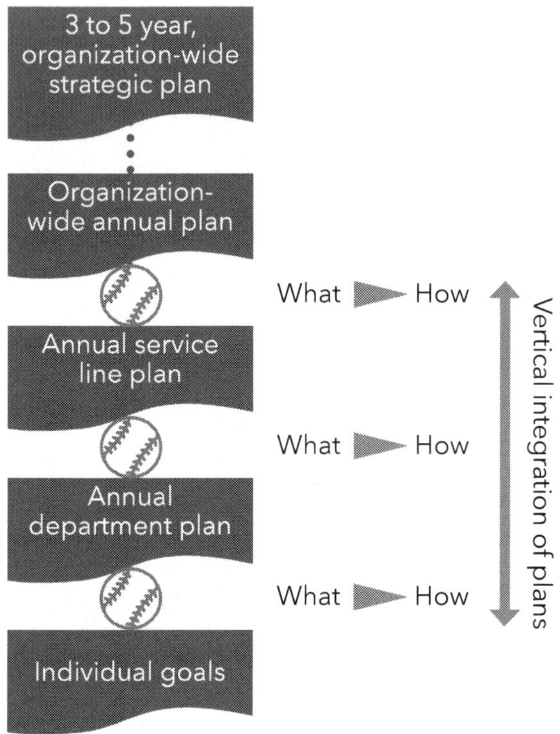

Figure 7: Catchball occurs throughout the organization as the annual plan is cascaded and translated all the way to frontline unit and individual goals.

During catchball, a leader describes and clarifies the *what* of the plan, including the organization's strategies, goals, metrics, and targets. Once those desired outcomes are clear, the question to the next-level leader is, "How can your part of the organization contribute to attaining these outcomes?" This begins the dialogue, the back-and-forth, on what the next organizational level can contribute in terms of initiatives and performance outcomes. This is a discussion about both projects and metrics. For example, a department leader might agree: "We can contribute to the length of stay reduction initiative by improving our discharge process to shorten the length of stay on our unit by half a day." More regarding the linkage of metrics to the strategy deployment process will be covered later in this chapter.

Catchball discussions typically occur from the top down in an organization to enable the logical deployment of the strategic plan. That is, catchball between executives and service lines are conducted before service line leaders conduct catchball sessions with departments. This is to ensure that the linkage and logic to the highest level of strategic goals is maintained. That is not to say, however, that higher-level catchball discussions cannot be reopened. Indeed, as catchball flows throughout the organization, it may be clear that plans discussed at other levels in the organization could benefit from revision given new information.

Critically important during catchball is for leaders within a division or service line to work collaboratively to determine what

Lessons from the Field

Rather than catchball, it felt as if the team was playing fetch with the corporate office when it came to annual planning and budgeting. The team was constantly chasing the many priorities being thrown its way. It took difficult conversations with corporate leaders before they understood the negative effect this was having. It turned out the corporate executives were not even aware of all the directives because there was no tracking and no effective communication. Nor had the leaders seen the demoralizing effect on other teams when they did not have a say in their own direction. Things changed for the better, and the site teams gained a voice in setting priorities on which to focus. It became acceptable to place projects on hold, sunset them, or cancel them altogether. The system instituted a process to make course corrections during the year. All parties met to discuss possible changes, understand the impact a change will have on other key initiatives, and agree on any changes before implementing them. Through this improved process, buy-in to the goals and initiatives increased, and goals were met more fully and more quickly.

can realistically be done to accomplish the strategic goals in the most optimal manner. For example, if one department or unit is struggling to resolve an important care-related issue, it might be best if they were not tapped to undertake something new until the existing issue has been resolved. Also important is establishing a means to conduct catchball across the organization. When catchball is only carried out vertically, disconnected silos of initiatives can proliferate. Looking across the organization will ensure that all relevant departments are contributing toward any given strategic objective without unnecessary duplication or sub-optimization of efforts.

The output of an effective catchball process is a strategic plan that has been cascaded to the frontline and coordinated across the width of the organization. Catchball helps create a detailed annual plan, optimized across the organization; applicable to everyone in the organization; and complete with projects, metrics, and targets for those metrics.

At the frontline level, supervisors and team leaders must work out the operational details to successfully implement the process improvement projects that support the initiatives or tactics as laid out by mid-level leaders. Once again, the principle of catchball applies to ensure that activities on the frontline are strongly aligned with organizational strategy and goals. This is critical since the frontline is where goals and plans are transformed into results on a daily basis.

Cascaded Metrics

Just as plans are cascaded through the organization in strategy deployment, metrics are also needed at all levels to ensure that progress is being made. Both leading and lagging indicators are typically discussed during the catchball process.

Lagging indicators are outcome measures that demonstrate performance results. They *lag* because they are generally measured after—sometimes long after—the action that produced them occurred. **Leading indicators** are real-time process measures of performance that predict overall performance. Leading indicators change before overall performance starts to exhibit any patterns or trends. They allow leaders and staff to make changes before an outcome is final. They provide an early warning of potential problems that can be addressed before overall performance is affected.

Lagging Indicators: Indicators that measure overall outcomes or results that are seen only after actions are taken.

Leading Indicators: Real-time process measures of performance.

To illustrate leading and lagging indicators, consider the example of an organization seeking to reduce hospital-acquired conditions. Using the Pareto Principle, the organization determines that the greatest number of infections are MRSA and C-difficile. The organization focuses on improving hand hygiene and room cleaning effectiveness as these interventions are proven to combat these types of infections. Hand hygiene and room cleaning are high-volume activities that occur many times a day in every hospital. The measurement of daily compliance to best practices in these activities generates leading metrics that can be studied, acted upon, and improved in near real time. The organization's hypothesis is that by measuring and improving these leading metrics, the lagging metrics of MRSA and C-diff rates will improve over time.

When cascading strategy, leading and lagging indicators are needed for every level of the plan. Figure 8 illustrates four examples of indicators that are cascaded from the system or organization-wide level down to the frontline. Although these examples show a linear progression for each metric, any metric can be fanned out through the organization as different areas determine how they can contribute to improve a higher-level metric.

Time	
Strategic Goal	Eliminate wait time to see a provider
System-wide metric	# of patients waiting for provider assignment in ED and Primary Care
Service line or care setting metric *Ambulatory*	Time to next available appointment
Department metric *Pediatric Clinic*	# of open slots for same-day appointments
Process metric *Pediatricians and Advanced Practice Providers*	# of providers with two slots open for same-day appointments

Cost	
Strategic Goal	Reduce expenses
System-wide metric	Salary dollars paid to contract staff
Service line or care setting metric *Hospital nursing*	Vacant positions
Department metric *Human resources*	Time to fill open RN positions
Process metric *Recruiters*	# of viable candidates provided to managers per week

Quality & safety	
Strategic Goal	Reduce readmissions
System-wide metric	# of all cause readmissions within 30 days
Service line or care setting metric *Primary Care*	# of diabetic patients readmitted within 30 days
Department metric *Family Medicine Clinic*	% of diabetic patients with A1C < 9
Process metric *Clinic Nurse*	% of patients referred to the diabetic educator

Experience	
Strategic Goal	Top decile performance in patient experience
System-wide metric	% of patients rating 9–10
Service line or care setting metric *Hospital Inpatient*	% of hospital inpatients rating 9–10
Department metric *Med-Surg*	% of call lights answered within five minutes
Process metric *Nursing staff*	Rate of hourly rounding per patient

Figure 8. Examples of indicators cascaded from the system or organization-wide level down to the frontline.

Through catchball and the cascade of leading and lagging indicators, staff members can then have very local and specific goals, with related leading indicators, that are aligned with the organization's strategic goals. To continue with the example of hospital-acquired infections, staff in environmental services might have a goal of >95% daily compliance with room cleaning standards as audited by frontline and mid-level leaders for environmental services.

For all cascaded metrics, it is helpful to use balancing metrics as well. Balancing metrics are measures that are not the focus of the improvement effort but are related. Balancing metrics track dimensions of performance that could be damaged in the metrics targeted for improvement are pursued single-mindedly without systems thinking. For example, a narrow pursuit to decrease turnaround time could lead to unintended deterioration of quality. In this case, the targeted timeliness indicator might be paired with a quality indicator to ensure that as timeliness improves, quality is maintained or improved as well.

Ongoing Review

A consistent, ongoing, and frequent review process demonstrates leadership's commitment to the strategic direction of the organization and the willingness of all leaders to provide support for this important work. If the review process is erratic or missing entirely, the organization at large will likely determine that this strategic work is not important. No matter how exceptional the preceding catchball and plan development processes have been, a weak review process will destroy progress toward the vision.

As with catchball, the review process should be thought of as a two-way dialogue. The objective is to openly, honestly, and transparently discuss how things are progressing. Where there are barriers, the review process provides the opportunity for leaders and staff at all levels to collaboratively problem solve on how to overcome them. Where the environment or conditions have changed and the plans are out of date, the review process can be used to update those plans.

Because circumstances can change rapidly and plans can quickly be derailed by the tyranny of urgent but not important events, those organizations that move consistently and quickly toward strategic goals tend to ensure that senior leaders review progress monthly. This monthly review can be done in a variety of ways. Often it is a combination of these review strategies that best ensures that every business unit is touched and supported at least monthly. The most powerful review methods are outlined below.

- Rounding review occurs when leaders and executive owners of strategies visit business units to discuss strategic progress. This rounding ideally begins at the strategy deployment board described in the "Make It Visual" chapter. This type of rounding is most effective when it occurs at least monthly in areas with high impact on the strategic direction.

- Open forum reviews are public reviews where all leaders and employees are invited to attend and all senior leaders are present. Generally some subset of business units reports each month on strategic progress. The goal is generally to have each business unit report at least once a quarter in this setting.

- Closed forum reviews with the senior leadership team may also be used for business units to report. This may supplement the open forum reviews.

- Ongoing one-on-one review and coaching of leaders by executive owners of strategies and leaders' leaders can occur as frequently as needed. These coaching sessions may occur as often as weekly in fast-moving business units.

In addition to these business unit and organization-wide reviews, the frontline conversations about strategic initiatives can happen weekly and daily in huddles and staff meetings. This is where strategy meets the road as plans and metrics cascade into everyday work processes.

Lessons from the Field

Nursing staff knew their executive team was sincere about the patient centeredness strategy when they heard the CEO participate in a discussion about patient falls in their unit. She knew how many patients had fallen in the past 12 months, when the most recent fall had occurred, and how long it had been since the last fall. Staff nurses were encouraged when the CEO asked their ideas on how to further reduce falls and expressed her pride in how much they had improved.

Annual Review

In addition to the ongoing strategic reviews that occur many times a year, the organization benefits from an annual review of the overall planning and deployment process. This review is intended to focus on both the results achieved each year as well as the planning, deployment, and review system itself so that it can be improved from one year to the next.

Through the process of deploying strategy via catchball and cascaded metrics, leaders can shift their focus to systems, structures, and actions of the people within the organization (collective–external). An inclusive and purpose-driven strategy deployment approach both demonstrates and cultivates a respectful and mission-centric culture (collective–internal). This transformative structural work builds on the personal development work described in Part 2.

Questions to Contemplate

1. How do I contribute to the alignment of all leaders and staff with our organization's priorities?

2. How do our strategy deployment and review processes reflect the structure and process laid out in this chapter?

3. How have I as an individual, and we as an executive team, narrowed our priorities to the vital few? Am I and are we focused on the most important things?
4. In what ways do I encourage staff to contribute to the strategic direction of our organization?

We should work on our process, not the outcome of our process.

—W. Edwards Deming (1990)

Focus on Process

> **Process**: A series of actions or steps taken to achieve a particular end.

A **process** is a series of actions or steps taken to achieve a particular end. Processes are the fundamental building blocks of healthcare organizations. Like DNA in a living organism, well-functioning processes in an organization are essential for outcome success and growth. In healthcare, processes are the vehicle to deliver services such as a clinical treatment or produce a product such as an X-ray image. The customer of a process may be external, such as a patient, or internal, such as another colleague or department. A process requires some combination of people, equipment, tools, techniques, and materials to meet the customer's need.

A focus on process requires all associates to see with new eyes. Rather than being distracted by individual incidents and anecdotes, a process focus drives one to think logically about the sequence, connections, frequency, and purpose of activities. However, a process focus does not land solely on a singular process. Processes do not operate in isolation and need to be considered in relation to other processes that affect or intersect with them. In other words, processes link to other processes and create systems. For example, to increase the volume and speed of inpatients through surgery is of no avail if the floor beds to receive these patients are mired in a sluggish or over-capacity inpatient bed turn process. Processes must fit together into a well-coordinated whole. Hence, a focus on process requires systems thinking as described previously in the chapter "Cultivate Systems Thinking."

A focus on process enables organizational improvement in two major ways. First, a process focus reduces blame in an organization, thereby creating a safe culture for improvement. Second, once leaders and staff members can see processes clearly, the path to improvement is visible.

Process Focus as an Antidote to Blame

Blame is a powerful destroyer of relationships and a barrier to improvement. The organization that seeks the *root who* rather than the *root cause* of problems actively encourages hiding and obfuscation. In addition, blame begets blame. When one is the object of blame, it is easy to react by attempting to shift blame to others. The hunt for a scapegoat rather than the root cause of a problem crushes thoughtful process and systems thinking. The honesty, transparency, forthrightness, and truth needed to fuel organizational improvement is rare in a culture of blame.

> *"I learned to shift from a focus on the root who to the root why."*
>
> -Jack Barto (2016)

In organizations that operationalize process thinking, everyone asks, "What happened and why?" and not, "Who did it?" Leaders in such an organization understand that the people who work in a system are supported or constrained in their performance by the processes that make up that system. That is not to say that individual efforts and employee skills do not contribute to the quality of outcomes; they certainly do. But talented and motivated workers who are put in a poorly functioning process cannot perform to the highest levels, nor can these workers feel proud and motivated about their work. In addition, by blaming—and perhaps eliminating—the worker without improving the process within which the problem occurred, it is most likely that the problem will recur when the next worker comes along.

In his leadership seminars, W. Edwards Deming ran his red bead experiment to highlight the impact processes have on the people who perform the work (Deming 1990). The red bead experiment involved a fictitious company that existed to produce white beads. A volunteer group of what Deming referred to as *willing workers* would dip a paddle into a box containing a mixture of white and red beads. Though customers only wanted white beads, a few defects (red beads) were allowed under performance standards. The workers' performance was carefully tracked. Invariably, a certain number of red beads would be drawn along with the white beads by every worker. Though Deming praised, punished, fired, and scolded the workers, their performance did not improve or meet the goal.

The lesson from this exercise is profound. The design and structure of an organization's work processes and systems are the primary drivers of performance. They are largely to blame if the outcomes and results are not as desired. Every process is perfectly designed to get the resulting outcome, and outcomes will not improve unless the process is improved.

Jack Barto, CEO Emeritus of New Hanover Regional Medical Center in Wilmington, N.C., tells the following story about the power of process focus and lack of blame (Barto 2016):

> *During one of my weekly rounds, the two co-managers of one of our nursing units took me aside and shared that a patient had acquired an infection. They were visibly shaken by this. The unit record of no infections was the best in our network. I told them not to worry, to finish out their day and go home to a nice dinner and relax. I asked that tomorrow they huddle with the unit's staff to let them know what had happened. Then they could form a small team to determine why it had happened and identify measures needed to prevent future infections. The managers did just that. These two managers also shared this incident and how I responded to their colleagues. I was proud of the managers and the unit. What I didn't realize until later was how the word had spread about my reaction – that I didn't become upset or mad and that I had asked them to identify and fix the problem and not the person. The spread of this story helped move our culture toward a process focus. It*

created a safe environment where staff were not afraid if they made a mistake.

Process Focus as a Path to Improvement

When leaders and organizations actively increase process focus and decrease blame, the stage is set for improvement, and much improvement is needed in healthcare. Healthcare processes are riddled with non-value-adding activities, unnecessary requirements, out-of-date restrictions, and other barriers that hinder performance rather than help.

Waste and complexity in processes grow simply due to lack of thoughtful attention. A new regulation comes along, and the process is patched to accommodate it. No attempt is made to think

Lessons from the Field

The medication dispensing cabinet in the Emergency Department (ED) frequently ran out of lidocaine, a topical anesthetic sometimes used when closing a wound with sutures. Frustrated by delays when they were out of lidocaine, the ED staff blamed the pharmacy, the department responsible for restocking the supply cabinet. The pharmacy blamed the ED staff for not properly scanning when they pulled lidocaine. The finger pointing was leading nowhere, so the ED and pharmacy leaders and staff observed the process. They discovered that the ED techs were following the correct steps when they removed the lidocaine, but the supply count did not decrease. With help from IT, it was determined that lidocaine was programmed as a medication only a nurse could pull. Because ED techs were not authorized in the system, the machine was not recognizing their lidocaine pulls. After discussions with the medical, pharmacy, and risk management teams, the ED techs were formally given access to pull the medicine, and the cabinets were reprogrammed. The team had moved from blaming each other to finding the root cause of the problem, which led to a fundamental process change and the elimination of one stressor from an already-busy ED.

holistically or systemically about how the entire process or system is affected by the singular change. This happens repeatedly until the process has been patched and duct-taped together into something that has no chance of operating efficiently or effectively.

As an organization seeks to drive the waste and complexity from processes, it is important to remember that although there are many improvement methodologies, they are not all created equal. Some ignore the study of process, and others consider it central to effective improvement. Select a method that is of the second variety. Ensure that any improvement method promoted across the organization has a process focus hardwired into it.

This chapter has continued the identification of externally focused development work for the collective members of the organization. These processes and competencies reside in what Anderson and Adams refer to as the outer game of leadership (2016, 30). These practices and competencies can be uncovered and improved upon in the individual–external and collective–external dimensions.

The questions that follow are offered to enhance your thinking in regards to how you respond to process failures.

Questions to Contemplate

1. When and how do I tend to lose a focus on process?
2. Where do I see blame occurring in my organization?
3. When do I tend to blame? How can I reverse my tendency to blame?
4. What tools, techniques, and approaches can I use to maintain a process focus for myself and encourage others to do so as well?

Seeing is believing.

–Anonymous

Make it Visual

> **Visual Management:** The ability to manage important work by sight.

Why do sports fans frequently look at the scoreboard when the action is clearly on the field or court? How does a traveler find the correct gate at the airport or know whether the flight is on time? How does a driver know when he can safely proceed through an intersection, how fast he's going, or how much fuel is left? How does a shopper know which supermarket checkout lane is open? The answer to these questions is **visual management**. Like the instruments on an automobile dashboard, the intent of visual management is to display information in an easy-to-grasp format within ready view of all team members.

> **Situational Awareness:** Being aware of what is happening to understand how information, events, and one's own actions will impact goals and objectives.

Visual management enables rapid recognition and comprehension of important information. Visual management creates a heightened sense of **situational awareness**. It also makes problems, abnormalities, or deviations from standards visible to everyone. When these deviations are readily apparent, corrective action can be taken to immediately rectify problems before they escalate.

Visual management is frequently used by leaders who are committed to improving the delivery of value to customers as well as enhancing staff engagement. Visual management helps create transparency in the things that matter most in running an effective team, unit, or department.

Lessons from the Field

The nursing team members were finding it difficult to keep track of whether methicillin-resistant Staphylococcus aureus (MRSA) tests had been performed upon patient admission and upon all patient moves from one unit to another. Tracking became easier when a unit clerk suggested placing a pink slip on each bedside chart to show dates and locations of each MRSA test along with the patient's MRSA status. The pink slips provided a visual reminder to ensure compliance with MRSA protocols as well as a quick way to view existing MRSA data.

Though there are many forms that visual management can take, two kinds of displays have proven particularly powerful in healthcare organizations: strategy deployment boards and daily management data displays.

Strategy Deployment Boards

Strategy deployment boards are so named because they facilitate line-of-sight from an organization's strategic plan through the service lines, departments, and ultimately to frontline work units and teams. They help leaders and team members see the alignment between a unit or department's activities and the organization's strategic goals. These boards help keep priorities clear and guide resource allocation for improvement work. In addition, they clearly communicate progress toward targeted strategic goals, including outcomes and project status. Finally, the boards serve to actively engage frontline team members in the mission, vision, and strategic direction of the organization.

Strategy deployment boards can be used at every level of a healthcare organization and in every business unit or department. This pervasive presence ensures that the strategic plan of the organization will be visible to every staff member in every part of the company. This high level of connectivity of strategy throughout the whole organization is described in greater detail in the chapter "Align Everyone with the Organization's Strategy."

Figure 9 illustrates an effective template for the core information to be included on a strategy deployment board. Generally, at any one time, a business unit will be working on only two to three strategies. Each of these strategies of focus will be represented on the board and would ideally include the following four components for each strategy:

- **History:** A key performance metric (KPM) that represents the desired performance outcome the business unit seeks to see improve through its strategic improvement work. This metric is most helpful when plotted over time on a run chart or control chart to make historical performance and trends highly visible.
- **Priorities:** Through Pareto or other prioritization analysis, this portion of the board displays the key drivers of performance for the KPM.
- **Problem Solving:** Documented improvement work for the leading driver of performance is posted on the board. This information is posted as soon as an improvement project is started and kept current through the life cycle of the work. This is a key way to keep staff informed of and engaged in improvement work in progress.
- **Process Metrics:** These measures are typically monitored frequently (hourly, daily, or weekly) and are used to track specific behaviors and process changes being tested and implemented through the problem-solving process. These are leading metrics that drive the lagging outcome metric displayed in the history.

Strategic Goal

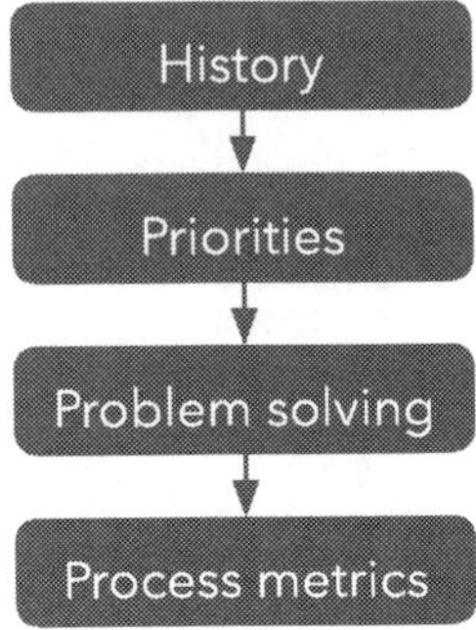

Figure 9: The flow from strategy to frontline improvement on a strategy deployment board.

For the maximum benefit to leaders and team members, strategy deployment boards may also contain a balanced scorecard or dashboard for the service line, department, or unit where the board is located. The scorecard or dashboard will allow all staff to see how the business unit is performing on a fuller set of key strategically and operationally driven metrics.

The exact layout of strategy deployment boards may vary between organizations, but it is important that the boards are standardized within an organization. Consistency in appearance and content will ensure that team members are working and documenting in a similar way and that everyone will be easily oriented to whatever board they see as they move throughout the organization.

Daily Management Data Displays

Daily management is continuous monitoring to ensure that work is performed in the right way and at the right time to meet the needs of patients or other customers. This routine surveillance allows leaders and staff to know if expected results are being achieved and, if they aren't, to adjust work processes in real time to positively affect outcomes. To support the work of daily management, highly visible and easily understood displays of real-time performance data are necessary.

Daily management data displays come in a variety of formats because the type of data needed to monitor and control processes at the frontline varies greatly from one business unit to another. In all cases, however, daily management data displays require Pareto thinking or prioritization to identify the most important metrics to monitor. Daily management metrics might be selected because they represent the processes and outcomes most critical to the core function of the business unit or most important to the customers. In addition, when processes are new or have been recently changed, it can be helpful to include metrics that will help ensure that the process changes are sticking and associates are not reverting to old behaviors.

It is also helpful to put daily management data displays as close to the work process as possible. This means that although a department or unit may have one strategy deployment board, the daily management data displays may be dispersed throughout the space. In a clinic, for example, if there is data that applies to the administrative staff at the front desk and clinical data that pertains to work done in the exam rooms, the administrative data should be put up front with the administrative staff and the clinical data put in the back with the clinicians. Placing the data close to the process and in full view of those who work in that process engages all staff in improving the organization by identifying and solving problems.

Updating daily management data displays should be made as easy as possible. There should be no need to use computers to generate glossy reports to post. In many instances, daily management data is manually recorded with markers on a dry erase board. The key is simplicity. Data displays that are easy to update and easy to read are critical to success.

The following are examples of effective daily management data formats.

Figure 10 is a situational awareness display at a hospital. It provides basic information about the unit at a glance so team members know what is happening on the unit at any given time.

UNIT SITUATIONAL AWARENESS

Date: 5/17	Census	47	Target	45

Safety Issues	# of Pts	Room Numbers
Sitters	1	09
Sick Patients	1	14
Security/Social Alerts	2	09 38
Isolation Alerts	5	08 32 33 38 42
Care Limitations	0	

Figure 10: A unit situational awareness board.

Figure 11 is an on-time tracking board that is used at the operating room control desk of a hospital. The charge nurse updates this each day to indicate which first case procedures enter the room on time and any reasons for delays.

OR Daily Management

Date: 3/23	Scheduled procedures	38	Target	40

Procedure room	On Time	Delay reason
1	Y	
2	N	Lab redraws
3	Y	
4	Y	
5	Y	
6	Y	
7	Y	
8	Y	
9	N	Surgeon late to pre-op
10	Y	

Todays % 80% Target 90%

Figure 11: An on-time tracking board.

Figure 12 illustrates a standard work tracking tool. In this example, a nursing unit at a children's hospital made changes to a key nursing care process. Standard work was created, staff members were trained, and the new process was implemented. This tracking tool was filled out by a charge nurse or supervisor who performed daily observations of staff members performing the newly designed process. If the randomly selected staff member performed the new process properly, a green dot was placed on the calendar for that day. If the staff member did not perform the new process properly, coaching was immediately provided, and a red dot was placed on the calendar for that day. A black dot was used to indicate that no observation audits were performed that day.

Month: Feb Standard Work Audit: CAUTI

Sun Mon Tues Wed Thurs Friday Sat

Figure 12: A standard work tracking tool.

Finally, Figure 13 shows how a nursing unit at a hospital tracked patient rounding. Patient rounding was an important addition to the daily responsibilities of leaders at the hospital, and this tool was completed by a charge nurse each day so team members could see how well they were doing with completing rounds.

Patient Family Rounding Target = 90%

Date	Total # of patients	Total # of patients/families rounded on	Percentage rounding completed
8/1	50	48	96%
8/2	49	49	100%
8/3	45	45	100%
8/4	45	45	100%
Week total	189	187	99%
8/7	45	43	96%
8/8	54	50	93%
8/9	55	0	0%
8/10	56	56	100%
8/11	63	63	100%
Week total	228	169	74%

Figure 13: A nursing unit at a hospital tracks patient rounding using a daily management tool.

Visual management techniques, including the use of strategy deployment boards and daily management data displays, support the improved delivery of value to customers as well as the enhancement of staff engagement. Visual management helps create transparency about the things that matter most in running an effective team, unit, or department. It engages everyone and encourages ownership of problems that must be solved. It enables everyone to do as W. Edwards Deming suggested in his 14 Points: "Improve constantly and forever the system."

Making systems, structures, and the process of improvement work visible makes explicit the collective–external dimension of Wilber's model. In each chapter of Part 3, these leadership practices are manifestations of the internal development work shared in Part 2.

Questions to Contemplate

1. How do leaders, staff, and providers in my organization gain situational awareness and know what's happening around us with respect to patient care and organizational functioning?

2. How am I currently using visual management?

3. How and where could I use visual management better to have a positive effect on leaders, staff, and customers?

4. How can I (and the broader leadership team) tie visual management to our organization's vision and strategy?

Where there is no standard there can be no improvement. For these reasons, standards are the basis for both maintenance and improvement.

–Masaaki Imai (2012, 56)

Promote Standard Work

> **Standard Work**: A clear, concise, and written description of how to perform a particular task so that the outcome will be safe, efficient, and of the highest quality.

Like visual management, **standard work** is a core tool for leaders who are committed to improving the delivery of value to patients and other healthcare customers. Standard work represents the best practice known at a point in time. Standard work in healthcare may include checklists, clinical pathways or protocols, standard operating procedures, flowcharts, or job breakdown instructions.

Despite the need for standard work, healthcare professionals frequently object to implementing it. There is ongoing discussion of whether or not highly educated and licensed professionals, in particular, should be asked to standardize work. The objections are often expressed as, "Every patient is different," "That's cookbook medicine," or "Healthcare is different."

The level of pushback on standard work in healthcare differs from how standardization is viewed in many other industries. In manufacturing, for example, standard work is generally non-negotiable and routinely deployed. It is time for healthcare to realize that standard work is necessary. The answers to a few questions are key to convincing the healthcare naysayers.

- Why standardize?
- How to standardize?

- Where to standardize first?
- When is standardization not appropriate?

Why Standardize?

Given the complexities of healthcare processes, standard ways to perform the work are necessary to achieve reliable and repeatable outcomes. For example, take the seemingly straightforward nursing processes in an emergency department. In the course of a week, there may be 10 nurses who rotate through the triage role and 30 nurses who rotate through the examination and treatment areas. If all of them have their own way of performing the work, that means there could be 300 combinations of how that work is done. Couple this with differences in the way individual physicians, techs, admins, and others do their work, and the variations grow exponentially. Without standardization, there is no way to

> "We have accumulated stupendous know-how. We have put it in the hands of some of the most highly trained, highly skilled, and hardworking people in our society. And, with it, they have indeed accomplished extraordinary things. Nonetheless, that know-how is often unmanageable. Avoidable failures are common and persistent, not to mention demoralizing and frustrating ... And the reason is increasingly evident: the volume and complexity of what we know has exceeded our individual ability to deliver its benefits correctly, safely, or reliably. Knowledge has both saved us and burdened us. That means we need a different strategy for overcoming failure, one that builds on experience and takes advantage of the knowledge people have but somehow also makes up for our inevitable human inadequacies. And there is such a strategy - though it will seem almost ridiculous in its simplicity, maybe even crazy to those of us who have spent years carefully developing every more advanced skills and technologies. It is a checklist."
>
> -Gawande 2009, 13

predict what the expected quality and patient experience outcomes will be. Without standardization, healthcare professionals cannot depend on colleagues' work nor know what to expect from each other. Predictability in process and outcome is not possible without standard work.

Further, recognizing problems is also very difficult without standard work. Errors and process failures can be obscured by the magnitude of variation in non-standard operations. Having standard work provides a point of reference for comparison to know when there is a problematic occurrence.

The rigor of discussing and creating standard work also provides a venue for the discussion of **best practices**. Though every organization is different and every patient is different, medical research, published studies, and local tests of change can provide helpful guidance on what works best in the majority of circumstances. Standard work, informed by internal and external expertise, becomes the keeper of the best ways we know to do work as of today.

> **Best Practices**: Methods or processes that are currently and generally accepted as superior to alternatives because they produce the best results.

Finally, standard work provides a foundation for improvement. The only way to see the result of a process change is to place it into a standardized and consistent environment. If the work is not standard when a change is made, it is impossible to know whether any outcome is a result of the changes made or other random changes in the environment.

How to Standardize?

Generally speaking, standard work is initiated while working to improve a process or stabilize an unpredictable or variable process. Both of these situations require process changes. Each time change is introduced into a workflow, leaders have an opportunity to promote standardization through documenting, training, and establishing interlocking layers of accountability. Each of these tasks is outlined below.

Documenting standard work

Standard work must be written to ensure it has a chance of becoming part of everyday practice. The writing of standard work is best done by those who are closest to, or work in, the process. Including these process experts in the documentation process ensures that the standard work is viable and clearly described. In addition, workers are more likely to follow standard work when they participate in developing it. This does not mean, however, that a leader should delegate the task of developing and writing standard work to frontline staff and then walk away. The leader has a critical role in coaching staff members as they become skilled and comfortable in writing standard work. By working with the staff, but allowing the staff to take the lead, a good standard work product can be gained, commitment to the standard processes grows, and the skills of all are enhanced.

Standard work is robust when it includes three components: what to do, how to do it, and why it must be done this way. Including all three components will result in standard work that is easy to be understand and likely to be followed. In particular, stating *why* steps and actions must be done in a certain way ensures that workers do not drift from the standard because they do not understand its importance. It is helpful for leaders to coach those developing standard work to address all three components.

The final step of documenting standard work is to perform a limited test in the real work environment before full deployment to the whole team. Testing may be done for a short time with only a subset of workers. Invariably during testing, some important detail will be brought forward that can enhance or change the standard work. The old adage of "pay it now or pay it later" applies here. Pay it now by testing and learning the effectiveness of a new standard work process, or pay it later in reworking and retraining staff.

Training to standard work

This is a step often given too little attention in healthcare settings. Leaders often assume that distributing a standard work document is enough to ensure the changes will be made. But understanding and committing to a new way of doing work requires more than the distribution of procedure, an emailed instruction, or a quick mention in a staff meeting. Instead, to increase success with implementing standard work, robust training is needed. A simple three-step framework known as behavior modeling is effective for standard work training:

1. Describe the work process.
2. Demonstrate the work process.
3. Practice the work process with immediate feedback.

The first two portions of this approach, *describe* and *demonstrate,* may be delivered in a number of ways: live, by electronic means, or by video. The third step, *practice*, must be done in a live setting so that a coach can provide immediate feedback. The feedback helps to prevent adoption of non-standard behaviors before they become habits. As a final tip, the success rate of the training will increase when learners can follow written standard work documentation as they hear about, see, and then practice the standard work process. This three-step approach to training standard work is adaptable to standing staff meetings, special meetings, and even competency fairs where staff work their way through a series of booths focused on various standard work processes. Finally, though a leader may delegate the actual delivery of standard work training, a leader maintains the accountability for the quality and effectiveness of that training.

Establishing interlocking layers of accountability

Training is not the end of the leader's role in standard work deployment. Leaders must recognize that a single practice experience in a simulated setting does not ensure the adoption in the real environment. Leaders must follow their workers' performance back to the frontline and observe. Is the standard work actually being deployed fully, or are there variances from the standard work? If there are deviations from standard work, the leader can return to the student mindset and ask why that is. The leader may find the standard work needs to be adjusted or there are barriers to adoption that require the leader's attention.

> **Leadership Standard Work:** The documented activities that leaders must consistently perform to ensure that processes run well, people are supported, and results are good.

As leaders at all levels work to ensure that those they lead are able to execute standard work, these leaders are creating interlocking layers of accountability for performance. This cascaded review and support for standard work is a component of what can be considered **leadership standard work**. Just as staff standard work defines expectations of frontline behaviors, leadership standard work defines expectations for leader behaviors. Leadership standard work outlines actions leaders consistently take to know how well processes are performing, identify problems, and initiate problem solving to take the team's performance to the next level.

With regard to the leader's standard work of sustaining staff standard work, leaders must identify how they will determine compliance to and the effectiveness of standard work. Usually this involves measuring and monitoring indicators that track the behaviors required by standard work and the resulting process performance. Process indicators are generally collected in one of two ways: through observation or by mining electronic systems. The monitoring of process indicators can provide evidence that standard work was fully implemented and, if so, if the change resulted in an improvement in simultaneously monitored outcome indicators.

As a leader monitors process indicators associated with standard work, there can be several signals in the data that lead to varying leader responses. These common signals and responses are outlined below.

Change in Indicator	Leader Response
Positive	Acknowledge the hard work of staff in implementing standard work. Celebrate the positive change in outcome indicators. Recognize and celebrate in a way that is meaningful to staff. Some examples include verbally acknowledging the results in daily huddles, visually calling out the improvement on the visual board, sharing the results with senior leadership, sending thank-you notes to individuals who helped lead the change, celebrating with food, or publicizing the improvement in organization communications.
Negative	Return to the student mindset to learn from team members about what is not working. Coach individuals who are struggling to comply with standard work. This will usually require observation to see what steps of the new process are challenging.
Both positive and negative	Identify and solve new problems that could not previously be seen because of the variation in how the work was performed.

Where to Standardize First?

Once a leader or organization commits to creating and implementing standard work, it can be difficult to know where to start. Healthcare delivery is complex and involves many processes. It can be daunting to prioritize the effort. It is helpful to begin with three to five processes to standardize, implementing one at a time. The following strategies can help decide where to start.

Focus on the customer

To focus on the customer, healthcare leaders must understand what needs their patients and other customers have and what services or products their organization provides to meet those needs. Using data, Pareto thinking, and problem analysis, leaders can identify processes that have a great impact on customers: those that most affect service, quality, cost, and time and provide value for the customer. These are the processes ripe for standardization. Standard processes result in reliable outcomes for the customer.

Align with strategic goals

After focusing on customer needs, it is useful to analyze processes against their impact on the strategic plan. This improves operations while moving the organizational vision forward. In essence, it provides a two-for-one return on time investment.

Analyze the current condition of work processes

The Joint Commission and other healthcare regulators suggest that organizations focus improvement efforts on processes that are high volume, high risk, problem prone, exhibit high unwarranted variability, or are critical but infrequent such that staff may be inclined to forget how to perform the work. These criteria are also helpful for identifying where to focus standard work. In addition, where standard work already exists, the assessment of whether that standard work is being followed and if desired outcomes are being achieved by that standard work can demonstrate where existing documentation of processes could benefit from review and revision.

When is Standardization Not Appropriate?

Not all work processes can be standardized. There are tasks, both clinical and non-clinical, that are non-routine and demand extensively developed technical expertise to deal with highly variable patient or environmental conditions. This *craft* work remains outside the domain of standardization. However, most workers in healthcare, including physicians, perform a mix of tasks that are suited to standard work and tasks that are not. Generic procedures, like surgery timeouts and IV insertion, can be standardized.

Standardizing processes in an organization is the beginning of improving performance, not the end. The goal of standardization is to stabilize a process such that outcomes are reliable and problems can be identified and solved, thus taking performance to a higher level. Standard work for staff members and leaders is not static. It must continually improve as the leader, the team, and the organization learn from improvement efforts. The process of developing standard work through staff involvement sets in motion new and trusting relationships between staff and leadership. This ultimately reinforces a healthy and vibrant organizational culture: the collective–internal dimension of Wilber's model.

Questions to Contemplate

1. To what extent does standard work exist within my own work and area of responsibility?

2. What steps can I take to determine what processes within my area of accountability are most in need of standardization?

3. How do I know if standard work is being effectively used to sustain process improvements?

4. How can I hold myself and the leaders who report to me accountable for both their own and their staff's standard work?

Surface problems when they occur, solve problems where they occur, sustain the improvement and share the knowledge.

–paraphrased from Steven J. Spear (2009)

Create an Organization of Problem Solvers

> **Problem Solving**: The act of defining a problem, determining its cause, identifying and selecting alternatives for a solution, and implementing a solution.

Ideally, problems are identified immediately as they occur. Then, identified problems are addressed quickly by those involved in and most knowledgeable of the process. Effective solutions that efficiently use resources are created. In this ideal world, all problem solvers use data and the scientific method to experiment with changes that are hypothesized to be improvements. Coaching spurs problem solvers to improve their skills along the way. Finally, when an experiment is successful, the change is hardwired for sustainment and spread across the organization so others can learn and benefit from it. Such an organization, sometimes described as an army of problem solvers, isn't just a theoretical ideal. Exemplary organizations throughout the world operate in this way.

Mobilizing every worker toward solving problems is a worthy but hefty goal. It requires attention to both individual and organizational issues. It requires resources. It requires constancy of purpose. It requires focused attention to the following key tasks:

- Adopt a standard **problem-solving** method.
- Set clear expectations about problem solving.

- Support everyone in learning the problem-solving method.
- Actively coach problem-solving efforts.
- Work ceaselessly to create a safe environment where problems can be surfaced.
- Take action on problems.
- Maintain a culture of continuous problem solving.

Adopt a Standard Problem-Solving Method

Senior leaders must decide to which problem-solving method the organization will commit. In healthcare, problem-solving methods are commonly known as improvement or quality improvement (QI) models. Though there are many viable problem-solving methods, it is critical that the organization adopt *one* model and standardize language and approach. This allows all workers to communicate quickly and work efficiently in solving problems, saving time and energy that could be lost negotiating which approach to use.

Helpful criteria for selecting a standard improvement or problem-solving method include the following:

- The method should incorporate a strong process focus.
- The method should explicitly call for root cause analysis.
- The method should encourage and incorporate the use of data for both baseline assessments and post-experimentation.
- The method should hardwire the scientific method into the approach.

Set Clear Expectations About Problem Solving

In order to create an organization full of problem solvers, it is important for leaders to be clear that everyone is expected to learn and use the organization's standard problem-solving process. This expectation must be clearly communicated by the senior executives to all staff, both leaders and non-supervisory personnel. As with any major initiative, this message is ideally communicated multiple times, in multiple venues, in multiple forms, both written and oral.

The expectation for staff involvement in problem solving may include targets for the number of problems that each leader or frontline team member will work on over a certain period. These targets might be set as monthly, quarterly, or annual goals. Both individual and team problem-solving efforts can often count against the goal. The purpose of setting such targets is not only to drive improvement but also to encourage skill development in problem solving.

Setting the expectation that everyone will participate in problem solving also requires leaders to adopt a new stance when problems are brought to them. When a team member brings a problem to

Lessons from the Field

A healthcare system was determined to train 80% of their employees in problem solving within three years. The executive team decided that the first group trained would be leaders and staff working on two key strategic initiatives: decreasing length of stay in the hospital and preventative care measures in the ambulatory environment. Leadership involved in the first training groups included the entire executive team, key physicians, and a vertical slice of the targeted improvement teams from the director level to the frontline workers. All participants were expected to complete several problem-solving projects during and immediately after the training. Completion of these starter projects and the related outcomes were routinely tracked and reported to the executive team. These early learners then moved on to applying their problem-solving skills to their assigned strategic priorities.

the leader, the employee often expects the leader to solve the problem, and the leader tries to solve it. After all, isn't it the role of the leader to be wise, powerful, and capable of solving all problems? In actuality, this is a recipe for disaster. In the healthcare setting, leaders do not have the knowledge or the time to solve every problem. If the leaders are the only skilled problem solvers, they become a bottleneck to improvement. Staff will eventually have little faith that anything will change and thus may not even bring attention to problems. In addition, every time a leader solves a problem for someone else, that leader has chosen not to develop the problem-solving skills of others. To grow an organization of problem solvers, a leader must choose wisely which problems to take on and which problems to delegate or coach others to solve. The inclusion of others in problem solving expands and accelerates organizational improvement and places problem solving back where it belongs: close to the problem.

Lessons from the Field

In one clinic, urine tests were conducted routinely on all patients with diabetes. Often, when medical assistants were rooming patients, there were no specimen cups available in the exam room. The particular medical assistant present at the time would walk down the hall to obtain a single cup so that the patient could provide a specimen. This occurred multiple times a day to multiple medical assistants. Meanwhile, the providers waited for the results of the specimen testing and each patient visit took longer throughout the day, resulting in providers leaving late and medical assistants working overtime. This went on for months while no one thought to problem solve regarding the issue of stock outs in exam rooms. While no physical harm occurs in this example, it highlights the cost of inattentiveness to problem solving.

Support Everyone in Learning the Problem-Solving Method

Creating an organization of problem solvers requires investment. Leaders often argue that there just isn't enough staff or time in the day to teach everyone to be a problem solver. This is akin to saying, "We have too many fires to extinguish. We don't have time to work on the prevention of fires."

Indeed, it is a leap of faith for leaders to commit resources to this learning and development effort. Leaders who make this commitment believe that the investment will return gain to the organization as small problems are solved before they grow into huge ones and that recurring problems will cease to cause damage and drain the organization of time and energy. These committed leaders also see that as problem-solving competency grows, fewer problems will require escalation up the chain of command. The result is that

Lessons from the Field

The manager of a large surgical services department welcomes each new employee with a problem-solving task. He asks each to think about a problem she or he is having at home and work through the organization's problem-solving method. Once the department manager has reviewed and coached this personal problem-solving effort, he asks the new staff member to identify some work problem he or she has seen as a result of bringing fresh eyes to the department. The manager then coaches the new associate through a second problem-solving effort. At the completion of these two starter problem-solving projects, the new employee is grounded in the problem-solving method and is inspired to continue identifying, studying, and creating solutions to workplace problems. Significant departmental improvements have been gained from just these initial improvement projects, and the department is alive with dialogue regarding how to continue improving.

leaders at all levels have more time to engage in coaching staff and addressing strategic rather than emergent issues.

To grow effective problem-solving skills among team members across an organization, a thoughtful, comprehensive, and written learning plan is needed. The plan should describe how every leader and each worker will learn the necessary skills. Formal classroom training for leaders and key support staff, if accompanied by real problem-solving projects, can accelerate the spread of the methodology. It is powerful for participants to solve at least one problem while in training, either independently or in a small group of no more than three people.

Some organizations have sufficient internal resources to support such an effort while others need external trainers and coaches to get started. In addition to classroom education, many staff may receive on-the-job training in problem solving. It is often the leaders who train their frontline staff in these tools. In addition, ongoing coaching, as addressed in the next section, is helpful to all.

Actively Coach Problem-Solving Efforts

Problem solvers benefit from coaches who have advanced problem-solving skills. Though an organization's first problem-solving coaches may come from a dedicated improvement support staff, ultimately all leaders at every level of the organization must become coaches to their direct reports. Therefore, leaders must grow their coaching skills in addition to their problem-solving skills. Admittedly, most leaders would hope to practice problem solving thoroughly first and then take on coaching others. In reality, however, leaders often have to practice and coach simultaneously.

> **Tollgate**: Planned points in the improvement process where work is reviewed and coached.

It is helpful for coaches to use **tollgates** with problem solvers. Tollgates are hard stops in the improvement process where the problem-solving project is reviewed and the problem solver is coached on completed work and next steps. Standardized tollgates ensure that coaches check in with problem solvers at frequent enough intervals that problem solvers do not proceed far down non-productive or frustrating paths. Tollgates can be helpful at the following stages of problem solving:

- When the problem statement, data, and current process have been defined.
- After analysis for root causes.
- When the change experiment is planned.
- When the new process is fully implemented.

Work Ceaselessly to Create a Safe Environment Where Problems Can Be Surfaced

For problem solving to become pervasive in an organization, workers must feel safe to surface and solve problems. A safe environment is enhanced when leaders respond in an open and respectful way to staff members who surface problems. A safe work environment must be addressed daily.

A clearly defined, standard process for problem identification also contributes to an environment where all staff members feel safe to speak up. Such standard processes do not have to be complex. Daily management, daily huddles, and process observation are relatively simple yet effective methods that leaders can implement to help make it comfortable for staff to surface problems. As described in the "Make It Visual" chapter, daily management is the disciplined, transparent, and visual tracking of meaningful measures of core processes or improvements for the purpose of understanding whether the team is meeting the customers' needs and following the standard work. A daily huddle is a quick conversation with the team to understand why performance is good or not. Process observation is an essential tool for supervisors and leaders to truly understand how a process is performing, validate whether standard work is being followed and is effective, and discover what problems exist that make it difficult for staff to meet customers' needs.

Take Action

Once problems are surfaced, they must be acted upon. When problems are identified yet fall into a black hole, never to be seen again, staff members quickly learn to remain silent. Non-response to problems leads to the belief that there is little reason to flag subsequent problems. Tips on how to effectively take action on problems include the following:

- Use visual management to track problems that are surfaced and their status.
- Observe the problem firsthand. Through direct observation, the leader deepens his or her understanding and reassures staff members of the value of their thoughts and ideas.
- Ask for staff members to be involved in solving the problem. Recognize their work by having them report on progress.
- When problem solving is assigned to staff, be explicit and vocal about the intent and commitment to coach the problem solvers.
- Huddle daily to follow-up on problem-solving efforts. This assures staff that problem solving is a critical component of the team's daily work and is not optional.
- Be transparent when a problem cannot be addressed immediately or at all. Pareto thinking causes some problems to take a lower priority. If range of authority puts some problems out of reach, or if strategic direction indicates that a certain problem does not warrant attention, the leader should thank the staff member who surfaced the problem and be honest and direct if it will not be addressed.

Maintain a Culture of Continuous Problem Solving

It is tempting to think of an organization of trained problem solvers as an end in and of itself. The goal is not to have 100% of the staff skilled in the method. The goal is to solve problems and enhance the organization's ability to meet customer expectations through process standardization and improvement. It is a never-ending journey.

There are three occurrences that can be expected as problem-solving capacity increases:

- As an organization gets comfortable with problem solving, more problems are likely to surface. This is to be celebrated as a sign of the culture becoming increasingly fair, safe, and improvement-driven.
- As an investment is made in people to grow their problem-solving skills, some will be ready to accept new levels of responsibility either inside or outside of the organization. As some individuals leave the organization, others will join and will need an orientation and development plan to grow their competency in problem solving. It is important to invest in systems and structures such as leadership orientation, coaching strategies, competency checklists for both problem solving and coaching, performance appraisal guidelines, and comprehensive job descriptions. This investment will ensure the sustainment of the problem-solving culture.
- A leader's competency with problem solving will evolve over time. In an organization that truly embraces rigorous problem solving, over time individuals will be able to deal with problems of increasing complexity.

The idea of an army of problem solvers speaks directly to Deming's teaching to put everyone to work in transforming the organization. This chapter sets forth to illuminate how inclusive problem-solving processes, operating in the realm of Wilber's collective–external quadrant, can shift organizational culture as realized in the collective–internal quadrant of Wilber's model. When leaders demonstrate belief that all organizational members are capable of improving care and service through robust problem solving, values and behaviors change in healthy ways. Deploying problem solving to where the problems occur shifts the locus of action from leaders to those who do the work. This underscores the importance of leaders learning the art of humility. As Schein states, organizational culture is "a pattern of shared basic assumptions that the group learned as it solved its problems of external adaptation and internal integration" (Schein 2010, 18).

Questions to Contemplate

1. What behaviors do I currently exhibit that inhibit the growth of problem solving in those who work in my areas of responsibility?

2. What can I do differently to foster an environment and mindset where problems are identified and solved as close to the work as possible?

3. Who on my team is ready to engage in problem solving? What do I need to do to support their problem-solving skill development?

4. Who on my team is ready to coach problem solving, and how can I support them?

[A]sking temporarily empowers the other person in the conversation and temporarily makes me vulnerable. ... But if part of the goal of the conversation is to improve communication and build a relationship, then telling is more risky than asking.

–Edgar Schein (2013, 9)

Develop Leaders as Coaches

> **Coaching**: A form of development in which an individual (coach) adopts a helping mindset to support individuals, teams, and ultimately organizations in achieving desired and measurable goals.

Throughout this book, **coaching** has been referenced as an integral element of leading an organization in continual improvement. In the most successful health-care organizations, the old leadership paradigm of *command and control* has shifted to the more effective model of *leader as coach*. Effective leaders embrace their role as coaches and adapt their behaviors to incorporate coaching to achieve organizational success. The practice of coaching demonstrates trust, mutual respect, empathy, and humility. Effective coaches actively listen and provide constructive feedback to support growth and development of the coachee. Coachees may be individuals or teams.

In the coaching relationship, the focus of the work is on the coachee and not on the coach. In other words, the customer of the work is the coachee. This is consistent with the philosophy of servant leadership as articulated by Robert Greenleaf (1977). The leader as coach is a servant leader, supporting staff and providers who in turn serve patients and the community.

To be fully functional as a coach, one must adopt a coaching mindset. In turn, a coaching mindset holds the belief that everyone is resourceful and wants to be treated as an engaged, whole person. A coaching mindset also propels a coach to seek understanding of the current context within which the coachee functions and to be openly curious about the coachee's world. Indeed, the coaching mindset is one of serving, learning, and mutuality in the relationship. A coaching relationship, when successfully developed, is not transactional. It is transformational. It is a mutually rich learning process for the coachee as well as the coach. In Wilber's model, the internal personal belief in others' capacity for growth drives the external actions of a leader to invest his or her time and experience in coaching others.

For a leader seeking to gain skill and comfort with the coaching role, it can be helpful to have a defined coaching process. Such a process is outlined below. It might be thought of as the standard work of coaching. The content of every coaching interaction will vary, but the coaching process model is robust enough to work in virtually all coaching situations. It can be applied to situations when coachees have a skill gap and are in need of personal development. It can be used when there is a relationship or political issue. The coaching process can be used to help move forward with improvement activity. It is a flexible process. The steps are outlined below.

Lessons from the Field

A health system decided that as they sought to transform their organization to a mission-driven, continuous improvement, patient-centric service provider, the role of leaders as coaches was critical. To reinforce the import of this leadership role, the term manager was eliminated from all job titles. In its place, the term coach was inserted. This symbolic gesture demonstrated the seriousness with which the executive leadership took the expectation that all leaders would see coaching as their primary role.

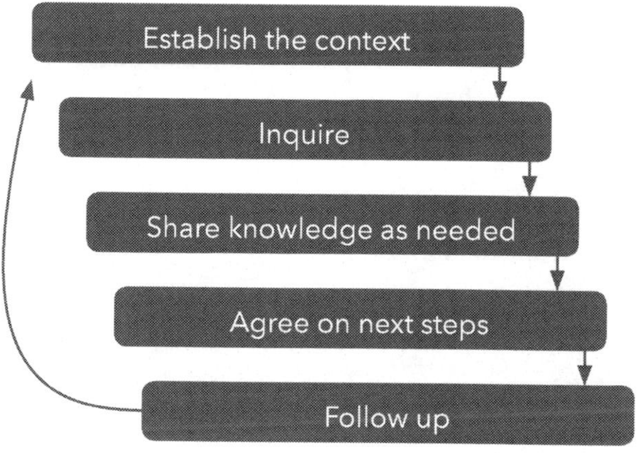

Figure 14: The coaching process.

Establish the Context

When setting the context, the leader as coach offers his or her motives for initiating the coaching conversation, creating an atmosphere of respect and trust. The leader clearly articulates an intent to support the development of the coachee's skills and abilities. This is a very different approach from either telling the coachee what to do or saying nothing and being dissatisfied with the results. The leader who verbalizes the rationale for coaching and acts consistently with the desired intent receives an added bonus of respect from those he or she serves. A foundation of respect drives leaders in understanding and responding to the coachee's strengths, weaknesses, biases, and behavioral tendencies. In other words, the leader as coach adapts his or her coaching to the unique needs of each coachee.

Establishing the context also requires the coach to have or develop an understanding of the current state of the unique situation and needs of the coachee. The effective leader as coach both understands the current state process in which the problem is occurring and how solving the problem serves to advance the organization's performance. As stated previously, observation coupled with inquiry, which is discussed in the following section, is a fundamental method for understanding the current state. Similarly, by observing the coachee in daily work, the leader better understands the coachee and can adjust his or her communication and leadership coaching to be more effective.

Inquire

To inquire is to question. When many think of inquiry, they think of the Socratic Method: a teaching approach where the teacher uses questions to direct and guide the learning of the student. However, the use of questions to delve into the coachee's situation is not an attempt to direct. It is an effort to create mutual learning.

> **Open Question**: A question that invites a full and detailed response rather than a one-word answer.

Open, neutral questions posed by a coach help the coach learn about the coachee, the coachee's world, and the presenting problem. This humble approach to questioning by the coach promotes learning for both the coach and the coachee (Schein 2013). It sets a tone of respect in the relationship. Both the coach and the coachee have important things to share.

> "I was committed to learning to improve my skills as a leader and coach. I was working diligently on how to ask questions through humble inquiry and resist the ingrained urge to tell people how to do something. I believed I was making good strides in my asking skills. Until one day during a team huddle, I was struck with an ah-ha moment as I asked the question, "Have you thought of doing____?" It was indeed a question, one I used routinely by adding what I thought they should do. However I had embedded a tell within my ask. That was a powerful moment for me...a rush of humility, as I recognized the way I was asking was taking away their opportunity to learn and grow".
>
> –Cindy Werkheiser (2016)

Through thoughtful questioning, the coach not only learns about the situation, but the coachee is spurred to think creatively about issues and potential next steps. The parties jointly explore positive next steps. The coach walks alongside the coachee as they progress together.

To inquire effectively as a coach requires attention to language and delivery. Not only must the questions be open and neutral, but they must be free of emotionally charged words. In addition, tone of voice and non-verbal behaviors can convey judgment, thereby shutting down the dialogue and the learning. This self-awareness is a pre-requisite to the external activity of coaching.

It is important to know that as a coach inquires, there is sometimes a point when asking further questions only serves to frustrate the coachee. It is important for the leader as coach to recognize when he or she doesn't know the next *good* question to ask and instead shares his or her knowledge with the coachee.

Share Knowledge as Needed

If the inquiry has gone well, the coachee and the coach have been working in tandem to uncover positive next steps. There are times, however, when the coach has information or skills that the coachee does not have. In these cases, the coachee will benefit from the experience and wisdom of the coach.

This is not the same as offering solutions. If a coach jumps too quickly to offer recommendations or countermeasures, the coach may have sabotaged the development of the coachee. When the coach moves too quickly to do for the coachee what the coachee, with coaching, can do for himself or herself, the coachee's development has been impeded. This can also reduce the coachee's willingness to engage and creates a culture of marginalization. In addition, this can create the potential for the coach to become a bottleneck as the coachee waits for the coach to provide all of the answers.

One other consideration to keep in mind at this point is that leaders as coaches often know *one* way to solve a specific problem and sometimes it is appropriate to share that knowledge. The challenge is for the coach to stay focused on collaborative learning and to avoid moving into the role of the one who has all the answers. In fact, *telling* in a coaching relationship may move the ownership for solving problems from the coachee to the coach. Although it is usually faster, and therefore tempting, to just tell the coachee what to do, spending extra time to discover the path together pays off in at least three ways. First, the coachee's skills expand. Second, the coachee may actually come up with a more innovative idea than the coach would have. Third, the coachee owns the next steps and is more committed to them.

There may be a toggling back and forth between knowledge sharing and inquiry. The coach may ask how the coachee may apply what was shared to deepen the coachee's understanding of the current situation. Sometimes what the leader has shared may not be helpful to the coachee; other times it may provide valuable insight to the coachee.

Agree on Next Steps

The fourth step in the coaching model is to come to a mutual understanding of the next steps to be taken. This establishes accountability primarily on the part of the coachee but also with regard to any actions the coach will take. It is important to clarify what next steps will be taken, who will take them, and by when will they be taken.

Follow-Up

The final step in the coaching process is follow-up. The coach can deepen the coachee's learning by engaging in dialogue about the results of the actions the coachee has taken. It is from the experiment of taking the next steps and seeing what happens that even more learning occurs. Unfortunately, it is common in healthcare that follow-up falls through the cracks, and a lack of follow-up can lead to missed opportunities for learning and improvement.

Leaders who coach perform a highly visible external activity that is informed by the leaders' personal values and behaviors. This activity directly influences the behaviors of not just the individual or team of coachees, but it also affects the organization's entire social system. It shapes habits and routines of everyone in the organization. Visible and active coaching encourages all to support one another; seek feedback; and strive together for personal, professional, and organizational development.

> "After 43 years of working as a CEO in hospitals, I believe the number one problem is that we don't coach to the fundamentals."
>
> -Art Gonzalez (2016)

In his Point 7, Deming challenged leaders to change the command and control leadership paradigm to a servant leader and coaching paradigm. Successful coaching behaviors necessitate a fundamental personal positioning in self-awareness, humility, and learning. Though developing skills in coaching is an ongoing personal process, noted in the individual–internal dimension, it manifests itself in the individual–external and collective–external dimensions. Visible coaching practices and behaviors are readily noticeable by staff. Such outward practices truly accelerate the desired cultural shift.

Questions to Contemplate

1. How often are my leadership behaviors consistent with the coaching model presented in this chapter?
2. In my coaching interactions, how do my questions and comments support the learning and growth of those I am coaching?
3. While coaching, what am I learning?
4. What do I need to do differently to promote coaching behaviors in myself and others?

Why are we here? We are here to come alive, to have fun, to have joy in work.

–W. Edwards Deming (1990)

Spread Joy in Work

Why focus on **joy** in work? Is this really important for leaders in today's hectic environment?

There are many benefits in an **environment of engagement** where there is joy in work. This kind of culture incubates the following:

> **Joy**: A feeling of well-being and gladness.
>
> **Environment of Engagement**: An environment where the conditions are ripe for all associates to give their best each day as all work together toward the aims of the organization.

- A sense of gratitude
- A focus on hope and possibilities
- A belief in abundance of goodwill rather than scarcity
- Satisfaction from serving others

These benefits highlight the absurdity of the common misconception that joy in work is inversely related to productivity and quality outcomes. It is not a tradeoff. It is not true that as joy in work goes up, performance goes down. In fact, the opposite is true. Joy in work is a resource for excellence. When employees' heads and hearts are captivated by purpose and hope, they can give no less than their best for those they serve inside and outside their organization.

To create an environment of joy and engagement, leaders can follow the interventional recommendations suggested in prior chapters:

- Provide aim and alignment.
- Focus on process.
- Make it visual.
- Promote standard work.
- Create an organization of problems solvers.
- Develop leaders as coaches.

These actions will counter the tendency of many organizations to confine the staff in a way that thwarts the calling and initiative of employees. Through these approaches, leaders can put right the unhappy legacy of systems that treat workers as assets to be tamped down and controlled. These actions can ignite the spirit of the good, decent, well-intentioned staff members who fill healthcare organizations.

There is one belief that, if held, can be a critical barrier to joy in work. That is the belief that there is a difference in what motivates people based on the organization chart. Many leaders see themselves as **intrinsically motivated** and **self-actualizing**. In other words, these leaders know that they personally *do* care about realizing their own full potential and contributing to society. However, many of these same leaders make the false assumption that this need for self-actualization is somehow connected only to the

Lessons from the Field

An inpatient floor team leader remarked that her job not only provided her with good pay and opportunities to contribute but had also deepened her broader life experience. She added that she had become a better person as a result of being part of an organization that believes in its people and provides the resources and coaching to continually improve the care it provides to patients.

top layers of the organization chart. They act as if those at the frontline of the organization, which is often at the bottom of the organization chart, are motivated only or primarily extrinsically by gifts cards, award certificates, or pizza parties. For an environment of engagement and joy in work to flourish, leaders must recognize that intrinsic motivation is not applicable to only certain titles within an organization. Most people respond to the call of self-actualization. Most desire to live fulfilling lives, to be the most they can be, and to contribute as much as possible. They want to connect with coworkers as well as customers. They want to contribute and to be valued. They want to learn and grow, both professionally and personally. And they want to be taken seriously.

Intrinsic Motivation: The desire to engage in a behavior that comes from within an individual and not from an external reward or punishment.

Self-Actualization: The desire to reach one's full potential: to be and contribute as much as one can.

A powerful way for leaders to create an environment of engagement, promote joy in work, and take workers seriously is to humbly learn about what is important to others. Former Toyota Chairman Fujio Cho famously said, "Go see. Ask why. Show respect" (Shook 2011). These three statements apply to learning about people as much as they apply to learning about processes. They are simple words with a powerful impact.

Respect: A feeling of deep admiration for someone elicited by their abilities, qualities, or achievements.

Cho's admonition to show **respect** is of particular importance. Respect for all people—patients, customers, providers, staff, leaders—is a key principle underlying effective leadership. But respect for staff is not about being friendly and nice, though those are not bad things. Respect for work associates is about challenging people to perform to their peak ability and ensuring they have everything they need to succeed. At its most fundamental level, respect means viewing and treating others as human beings. It means making every effort to understand each other's needs and desires and doing one's best to build mutual trust. It means recognizing people's knowledge, skills, and abilities, as well as the talent they can contribute, and creating an environment where everyone is encouraged to solve problems. And it means stimulating personal and professional growth, sharing opportunities for development, and maximizing the performance of individuals and teams. It means seeing others as trees and not a forest.

To show respect, humbly learn, and promote a joyful and productive workplace, leaders might maintain an active dialogue with those they lead regarding the following topics:

- The positive differences made by individuals and teams for customers, co-workers, and the community
- What team members do to make the organization better
- How well the organization and its leaders listen to employees and customers
- The level of autonomy and control that associates feel at work

Lessons from the Field

The executives at a health system felt so strongly about creating a culture of respect that they instituted a corrective action process (CAP) for disrespectful events. They did this in the same spirit of the organization's CAPs for sentinel events affecting patient safety. Any disrespectful event was documented and analyzed to determine what happened, to evaluate why it happened, and to ensure appropriate countermeasures were taken to prevent future occurrences.

- What additional support—information, education, tools, or systems—is needed to serve customers and peers well
- How workers are challenged and provided opportunities to learn and grow
- How the team could better share and celebrate successes

Joy in work! Such an outcome is the culmination of Deming's 14 Points. He believed that by respectfully engaging everyone in the improvement journey, the ultimate performance of the organization (system) could be achieved while individuals developed and flourished as well. This is why we close out Part 3 with this chapter. We believe that by seeking development within and across all four of the integral model's quadrants, true, sustainable engagement of everyone within the organization is possible. There can be a palpable shift within the collective membership of the organization when team members feel joy in their work. Hence, this deeply shifts how we personally lead and how the organization improves. This is the essence of a healthy organizational culture.

This list of questions are the last we pose, yet we are confident they will not be the last you ask of yourself.

Questions to Contemplate

1. How am I as a leader contributing to creating a workplace of engagement?
2. How do I as a leader provide opportunities for employees to learn, grow, and be challenged?
3. What leadership behaviors do I demonstrate to others to show that I care about them as people?
4. How do I foster an environment where people care about each other?

Coda

Epilogue

As you read the previous chapters and worked through the chapter questions, we hope you were provoked in some manner—that there was something you saw in the mirror of your own leadership behaviors and actions, as well as the systems and processes you have instituted, that appeared out of focus or off kilter. We hope you saw in yourself something you want to change. It is through these feelings of dissonance that we learn and grow. It is the distance between our current reality and desired vision, and the *dis-ease* we are not willing to tolerate, wherein real personal and organizational transformation occurs.

Over our many years working inside organizations and serving as external change agents, we too have been confronted by our rightness: our desire to have it our way so we are comfortable. The challenges have been many, we have overcome many, but we have many more to address. We have realized that leading improvement and organizational transformation is a journey propelled by curiosity, honesty, a willingness to let go, and a proclivity for purposeful action.

That is the spirit in which we wrote this book. Our intent was to share our learning as well as the learnings from successful transformational leaders with whom we have had the pleasure of working. The leaders with whom we have worked and coached have had similar experiences. All have had flashes or recognition when, like the cartoon character Pogo, we have met the enemy and he is us (Kelly 1972).

In these leadership and organizational experiences, leadership intent has been present, at least to some degree. The chosen method for improvement has demonstrated effectiveness in other settings. Why not here? The launch of the transformational engagement has been thoughtful, at least in some cases. However, the results achieved did not match the results desired. Though we, as a collective of experiences in this realm, do not have hard statistics, we can vouch for the approximate 30% success rate for intended transformational success.

We contend and have attempted to articulate that the failure for transformation is a failure in viewing the required changes in a holistic way. Using Wilber's Integral Theory model along with Robert (Bob) Anderson's helpful refinements, we framed the leading of continuous improvement and organizational transformation through the four quadrants of Wilber's model: look internally at *I* and *we* as you also look externally at interpersonal skills and behaviors as well as structure and systems.

The many available books on change provide useful tools and techniques, and many are worth studying and applying. However, we also believe successful change journeys are catalyzed not from the outside in but rather from the inside out. This starts with the deep introspective process of exploring our self. We ask, "What is important to me?" From this question and the others articulated in this book, we initiate our own personal development. It is in this space that we begin to redefine who we want to be and how we want to *show up*. The disciplined process of increasing self-awareness through self-reflective practices is critical to the learning process of the leader. This is ground zero for the change process.

Building upon this deeper personal introspection, we challenge how outward behaviors positively and negatively impact the realization of both personal and organizational vision. This stage is the actual behaviors we exhibit to others within the change process. This is how others see us. This is how we motivate, coach, and develop others in the organization. It is through our behaviors and actions that new individual skills and organizational capabilities are realized. New interpersonal skills begin to take root in the organization. What emerges are new ways of relating to one another and addressing problems.

As we challenged *who I am*, we also challenged *who we are* and *how we work together*. The approach to solving problems begins to shift. We shift from blaming *who* to seeking *why*. Jack Barto (2016) shifted from finding the *root who* to finding the *root why* a couple of years into his personal and organizational transformation journey. This may seem minor or inconsequential; however, these subtle shifts in leader behaviors and expectations initiate new stories told throughout the organization. These stories spread the change at an organic level. People at the frontline realize that they are being given permission and power to address problems, to use their own individual and—more importantly—collective genius to address problems that impact their work life and the customer experience.

The adage that it takes three to five years to change an organization's culture may or may not be true. We believe it will never change until leaders make a personal commitment to change and seek to lead these changes in all facets of their organization. The changes start small and within pockets of the organization. With the right leaders nurturing and developing deliberate systemic and structural changes, these small pockets begin to spread. These early adopters become the models for change, exemplifying the new leadership behaviors and ways of doing the work.

This idea was perhaps best expressed by Katie Knodel-Kummer (2016): "Go slow to go fast, start small with a few priorities, do not expect this kind of a transformation to occur overnight, and practice before deploying."

Creating an inclusive planning and deployment process with purpose and vision, in conjunction with a management system that makes transparent to all the focus on process improvement and problem solving, anchors the individual and collective behavior changes.

What we have shared and discussed—from self-awareness, purpose and vision, learning, and systems thinking in Part 2 and the system, structures and processes of Part 3—proceed from the fundamental reason for embarking on a continuous improvement transformation: our customer—the patients and their family members and the larger community, as well as our healthcare colleagues. The customer is the reason for our very existence as leaders of healthcare organizations. System and process improvement starts with a shift in how we relate to and interact with our customers. This shift requires us as leaders to redefine the relationship, seeking deeper understanding through dialogue while shifting the center of power from me, an ego-centric approach, to us, a mutually beneficial relationship.

Successful change begins with personal transformation, creating the possibility of organizational change, which is fully realized in organizational transformation. In the true spirit of continuous improvement, we acknowledge we are works in progress. If we consciously choose to take this journey of continual learning with the destination somewhere over the horizon, we will be surprised, enriched, and gratified. The contemplative questions we posed at the end of each chapter are our best in this moment. You may have better questions. Either way, challenge yourself by considering the questions. Pose new ones. Continually hold the mirror to yourself.

Celebrate even the smallest of positive changes in you and your organization. This holistic approach is challenging and fraught with setbacks. The act of celebrating provides the opportunity to pause, catch your breath, and begin to solidify the learning and new level of performance.

Finally, we suggest you follow, as we do, this advice for leaders.

> *Become a learner. Be patient, and open yourself up to new ideas. Coach and learn from others. Practice what you are learning. Tap into your employees and nurture the relationships. Finally, go to see the work.*
>
> *–Art Gonzalez (2016)*

Acknowledgements

There are many people to name and thank for an endeavor such as this. We feel compelled to acknowledge our current and former colleagues as well as our current and former clients. Words cannot fully convey the pride, respect, and admiration we have for each of you. Walking this path with you reminds us daily that healthcare is a calling rather than an occupation. All of us have been drawn to health professions because we want to help people and enrich their lives. We want to heal individuals while achieving a bigger purpose for our society. We will forever cherish the opportunities we have had to work with such outstanding people. You exemplify the qualities of passion, inquiry, competence, and integrity. Your influence on us profoundly shaped the perspectives that we shared in this book.

We would also be remiss if we did not single out a few individuals for their particularly weighty influence on us and this book. The first is Art Gonzalez. A former President/CEO of Denver Health, Hennepin County Medical Center, and several other hospitals and health systems across the country, Art ranks among the finest leaders and deepest thinkers with whom any of us has ever worked. Although we have served Art as consultants over the past 30 years, he was usually ahead of us in terms of his thinking about leadership, continual improvement, and everything else. We are honored to call Art a colleague and look forward to every opportunity to engage with him.

Next is Jack Barto, CEO Emeritus of the New Hanover Regional Medical Center (NHRMC) in Wilmington, North Carolina. Jack led NHRMC for more than 13 years, beginning his tenure with a singular vision: to be patient and community-centric. Through this transformational journey, Jack created an empowered culture that truly provides unparalleled services to the Wilmington region. In our many years of working with Jack and his leadership team, we have learned as much from them as they have learned from us. It was, and remains, an authentic collaborative relationship.

Third is Robert J. Anderson, Founder and Chairman of The Leadership Circle. Bob's research and work in leadership transformation has inspired our own approach. His work is underpinned by the belief that cultural change requires leaders to gain a deeper understanding of themselves, the world, and their relationship to others in order to embody and lead toward the desired culture. This deeper, longer-term work is what Bob's Leadership Circle Profile brings to the table.

We would also like to acknowledge Dr. Timothy Johnson, the President/CEO of the Mayo Clinic Health System–Franciscan Health (MCHS–FH) in LaCrosse, Wisconsin. Tim is such an embodiment of a servant leader that Robert Greenleaf must have had him in mind as he created the archetype. One of the humblest people we have ever known, Tim's enduring mark on MCHS–FH is his unequivocal and unwavering dedication to serving people in the southwest Wisconsin region. This mindset manifests itself every day through every decision and every action taken by the compassionate people at MCHS–FH.

Our list of influencers would be incomplete without Charles Hagood. An engineer, entrepreneur, and dear friend, Charles is a man with a heart of gold who is passionate about improving healthcare. He was instrumental in bringing all of us together, constantly pushed us beyond what we were currently doing, and challenged us to think beyond any specific methodology. The annual hoedown at his farm each fall was as entertaining as he was. Although we've managed to stay in touch with Charles since our paths diverged, we dearly miss our more frequent interactions with him.

Finally, we would like to acknowledge those who read drafts and contributed content ideas to this book. Those individuals include

Terry Howell, Marshall Leslie, Richard Tucker, and Sharon Benjamin.

Throughout this book, we have used quotes from those we interviewed and stories of what we have learned across our careers. While quotes were attributed, client stories were kept anonymous. Although credit for this book is to be shared with many, all errors and omissions are entirely our own.

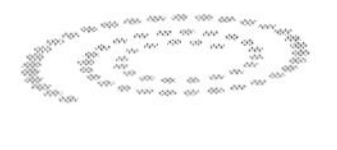

References

Anderson, R.J., & Adams, W.A., 2016. *Mastering Leadership*. Hoboken, NJ: John Wiley & Sons Inc.

Argyris, C., 1990. *Overcoming Organizational Defenses.* Needham Heights, MA: Allyn and Bacon.

Argyris, C., 1991. "Teaching Smart People How to Learn." *Harvard Business Review*, 69 (May–June), 99–109.

Barto, J., 2016. Personal communication: Interview with William Kirkwood. CEO Emeritus, New Hanover Medical Center, Wilmington, NC.

Bennis, W., 2009 (4th Ed.). *On Becoming a Leader*. Philadelphia, PA: Basic Books.

Block, P., 1993. *Stewardship: Choosing Service Over Self Interest.* Oakland, CA: Berrett-Koehler Publishers.

Brown, B., 2010. *The Gifts of Imperfection: Let Go of Who You Think You're Supposed to Be and Embrace Who You Are.* Center City, MN: Hazelden Publishing.

Covey, S., 2004. *The 7 Habits of Highly Effective People: Powerful Lessons in Personal Change*. New York: Free Press.

Deming, W.E., 1986. *Out of the Crisis*. Cambridge, MA: The MIT Press.

Deming, W.E., 1993. *The New Economics for Industry, Government, and Education*. Cambridge, MA: Massachusetts Institute of Technology Center for Advanced Engineering.

Deming, W. Edwards, 1990. *Quality, Productivity and Competitive Position.* Seminar presented January 30.

Drucker, P., 1999. "Managing Oneself." *Harvard Business Review*, 77 (Mar–Apr), 64–74.

Drucker, P., 1963. "Managing for Business Effectiveness." *Harvard Business Review*, 41, no. 3 (May), 53–60.

Gawande, A., 2009. *The Checklist Manifesto*. New York: Metropolitan Books.

Gizdic, J., 2016. Personal communication: Interview with William Kirkwood. CEO, New Hanover Regional Medical Center, Wilmington, NC.

Gonzalez, A., 2016. Personal communication: Interview with William Kirkwood. Retired CEO, Denver Health, Denver, CO.

Greenleaf, R., 1977. *Servant Leadership: A Journey into the Nature of Legitimate Power and Greatness*. Mahwah, NJ: Paulist Press.

Howell, W.T., 2016. Personal communication: Interview with Maureen Sullivan. Senior Principal, Vizient, Irving, TX.

Imai, M., 2012 (2nd Ed.). *Gemba Kaizen: A Commonsense Approach to a Continuous Improvement Strategy*. New York: McGraw-Hill Professional.

Kaplan, R., & Norton, D., 2001. *The Strategy-Focused Organization: How Balanced Scorecard Companies Thrive in the New Business Environment.* Boston, MA: Harvard Business School Publishing Company.

Kearns, H., 2015. *The Imposter Syndrome: Why Successful People Often Feel Like Frauds*. South Australia, Australia: Thinkwell.

Kegan, R., & Lahey, L.L., 2001. *How the Way We Talk Can Change the Way We Work.* New York: Jossey-Bass.

Kegan, R., & Lahey, L.L., 2009. *Immunity to Change: How to Overcome It and Unlock the Potential in Yourself and Your Organization.* Boston, MA: Harvard Business School Publishing Corporation.

Kelly, W., 1972. *Pogo: We Have Met the Enemy and He Is Us.* New York: Simon & Schuster.

Kirkwood, W., 2003. "The Current State of the Patient Care Nurse's Vocational Calling." Doctoral Dissertation. Cincinnati, OH: The Union Institute and University.

Knodel-Kummer, K., 2016. Personal communication: Interview with Blair Nickle. Director of Strategy and Performance Improvement, Alliance Health System, Morganville, NJ.

Kotter, J., 1985. *Power and Influence: Beyond Formal Authority.* New York: Free Press.

Mann, D., 2015 (3rd ed.). *Creating a Lean Culture: Tools to Sustain a Lean Conversion.* Boca Raton, FL: CRC Press.

Marsalis, W., 2005. *To a Young Jazz Musician: Letters From the Road.* New York: Random House Trade Publications.

Maslow, A., 1954. *Motivation and Personality.* New York: Harper & Brothers.

Molinsky, A., 2016. "Everyone Suffers From Imposter Syndrome: Here's How to Handle It." *Harvard Business Review*, July 7. https://hbr.org/2016/07/everyone-suffers-from-imposter-syndrome-heres-how-to-handle-it (accessed June 16, 2018).

Porter, M.E., 1996. "What Is Strategy?" *Harvard Business Review*, 74 (Nov–Dec), 61–78 .

Saint-Exupéry, A., 1943. *The Little Prince.* Boston, MA: Mariner Books.

Schein, E.H., 2010 (4th Ed.). *Organizational Culture and Leadership*. San Francisco, CA: Jossey-Bass.

Schein, E.H., 2013. *Humble Inquiry: The Gentle Art of Asking Instead of Telling*. San Francisco, CA: Barrett-Koehler Publishers Inc.

Senge, P., 1990. *The Fifth Discipline: The Art and Practice of the Learning Organization*. New York: Doubleday/Currency.

Senge, P., Kleiner, A., Roberts, C., Ross, R., & Smith, B., 1994. *The Fifth Discipline Fieldbook*. New York: Crown Business.

Shook, J., 2011. "How to Go to the Gemba: Go See, Ask Why, Show Respect." Lean Enterprise Institute. www.lean.org/shook/DisplayObject.cfm?o=1843 (accessed June 16, 2018).

Short, R.R., 1998. *Learning in Relationship: Foundation for Personal and Professional Success*. Bellevue, WA: Learning in Action Technologies Inc.

Spear, S.J., 2009. *Chasing the Rabbit: How Market Leaders Outdistance the Competition and How Great Companies Can Catch Up and Win*. New York: McGraw-Hill.

Training for Warriors, 2011. Ancora Imparo. www.trainingforwarriors.com/ancora-imparo (accessed June 16, 2018).

Weick, K.E., & Sutcliffe, K.M., 2015 (3rd Ed.). *Managing the Unexpected: Sustained Performance in a Complex World*. Hoboken, NJ: John Wiley & Sons Inc.

Weir, K., 2013. "Feel Like a Fraud?" *gradPSYCH Magazine*. www.apa.org/gradpsych/2013/11/fraud.aspx (accessed June 16, 2018).

Werkheiser, C., 2016. Personal communication: Interview with Maureen Sullivan. VP of Service Excellence, Monroe Clinic, Monroe, WI.

Wheatley, M.J., 2005. *Finding Our Way: Leadership for an Uncertain Time*. San Francisco, CA: Berrett-Koehler Pub. Inc.

Wheatley, M.J., 2006 (3rd Ed.). *Leadership and the New Science: Discovering Order in a Chaotic World.* San Francisco, CA: Berrett-Koehler Publishers.

Wilber, K., 2016. *Integral Meditation: Mindfulness as a Way to Grow Up, Wake Up, and Show Up in Your Life*. Boulder, CO: Shambhala Publications Inc.

Wilde, K., 2016. Personal communication: Interview with Maureen Sullivan. CNO, Hennepin County Medical Center, Minneapolis, MN.

Influencers

The following, in alphabetical order, are additional visionaries who have heavily influenced our thinking and approach.

Chris Argyris. Argyris was driven by a fundamental faith in human nature, and his seminal work on learning organizations has profoundly shaped our thinking and approach (Argyris 1991). Argyris argued that organizations depend on people and that personal development is related to work. Argyris believed that many organizations stand in the way of people fulfilling their personal and organizational potential.

Warren Bennis. Bennis is widely regarded as a pioneer in the contemporary field of leadership studies. His work on group behavior in the 1960s foreshadowed today's move toward less hierarchical, more democratic, and more adaptive institutions (Bennis 1989).

Peter Block. Block's perspective on choosing service over self-interest is an underlying theme in our book. His notion of stewardship honors the leadership's responsibility to use its power with compassion and grace and to pursue purposes that transcend short-term self-interest (Block 1993).

Brené Brown. Brown researches vulnerability, shame, and empathy. Her work is broadly applicable to leadership and personal development and brings richness to the concepts of self-awareness and humility (Brown 2010).

Robert Greenleaf. Greenleaf turned leadership thinking upside down when he introduced the concept of servant leadership (Greenleaf 1977). Servant leadership is based on the belief that the needs of followers are holy and legitimate and that a leader's use of power arises from the consent of the followers. Servant leadership focuses on the care taken by the servant to make sure other people's highest-priority needs are being served.

John Kotter. Kotter introduced the notion that power is embedded in the interdependencies of relationships (Kotter 1985). The greater the dependence, the more important the relationship. Kotter also presented organizations as complex systems that require leaders to understand power and influence.

David Mann. Mann's work on developing a Lean culture provides the key to sustaining Lean transformations via the Lean Management System (Mann 2015). While Mann's original book focused primarily on manufacturing, subsequent editions provide case studies with application to healthcare.

Abraham Maslow. Maslow's renowned hierarchy of needs continues to be a mainstay in organizational psychology (Maslow 1954). Despite the lack of empirical support for the hierarchy, its popularity is largely attributed to the fact that it just makes sense.

Edgar Schein. Schein was one of the first scholars to describe the importance of understanding organizational culture (Schein 2013). He argued that culture is the single most important source of information and understanding in organizational existence. Like the construct of personality, culture has powerful behavioral and attitudinal effects.

Karl Weick. Weick is one of the most prolific organizational theorists of all time. He introduced into organizational studies the concepts of loose coupling, mindfulness, sense making, and enactment (Weick & Sutcliffe 2015). He has profoundly influenced the way we think about thinking. In addition, his Organizational Information Theory provided much of the foundation for the study of high-reliability organizations.

Margaret Wheatley. Wheatley forged new ground in organizational and leadership theory through the integration of history, spiritual practices, and new sciences such as chaos theory and quantum physics (Wheatley 2006). Her work and writing has served to broaden the view of what it means to be an effective leader and an effective organization.

Self Awareness Tools, Methods, and Approaches

Journaling and Mindfulness

https://gratefulness.org/practice/practice-space/

This site provides a variety of journaling and mindfulness practices along with videos, suggested articles, and books.

Feedback Analysis

Peter Drucker developed feedback analysis. It is a process of comparing results anticipated from a decision or action to the actual results. It is detailed in the following article.

- Drucker, P., 1999. "Managing Oneself." *Harvard Business Review*, 77 (Mar–Apr), 64–74.

Left-Hand Column Exercise

This technique was created by Chris Argyris (1990) and popularized by Peter Senge (1990). It is intended to enable individuals to surface assumptions that operate below a conscious level but influence personal actions and reactions. An excellent guide to using this technique can be found in the work cited below.

- Senge, P., Kleiner, A., Roberts, C., Ross, R., & Smith, B., 1994. *The Fifth Discipline Fieldbook.* New York: Crown Business.

Immunity Mapping

Robert Kegan and Lisa Laskow Lahey developed immunity mapping to explore why individuals don't reach their personal goals even though they state commitment to them. Their immunity mapping technique helps uncover the basic beliefs and assumptions that constrain or prevent personal progress. The technique is described in chapter 2 of the reference below.

- Kegan, R., & Lahey, L.L., 2009. *Immunity to Change: How to Overcome It and Unlock the Potential in Yourself and Your Organization.* Boston, MA: Harvard Business School Publishing Corporation.

Additional Resources

The following sources provide multiple lessons, exercises, and tools for individual and group learning.

- Short, R.R., 1998. *Learning in Relationship: Foundation for Personal and Professional Success.* Bellevue, WA: Learning in Action Technologies Inc.

- Liberating Structures: www.liberatingstructures.com.

Recommended Readings

We strongly recommend these exceptional works to anyone interested in expanding his or her leadership horizons, and we believe you'll find them as stimulating and inspiring as we have. Some are new. Some have been around a time. All are classics.

- Anderson, R.J., & Adams, W.A., 2016. *Mastering Leadership.* Hoboken, NJ: John Wiley & Sons Inc..
- Argyris, C., 1991. "Teaching Smart People How to Learn." *Harvard Business Review*, 69 (May–June): 99–109.
- Bennis, W., 1989 (1st Ed.). *On Becoming a Leader.* Reading, MA: Addison-Wesley Pub. Co.
- Block, P., 1993. *Stewardship: Choosing Service Over Self Interest.* Oakland, CA: Berrett-Koehler Publishers.
- Brown, B., 2012. *Daring Greatly: How the Courage to be Vulnerable Transforms the Way We Live, Love, Parent, and Lead.* New York: Penguin Random House.
- Greenleaf, R., 1977. *Servant Leadership: A Journey into the Nature of Legitimate Power and Greatness.* Mahwah, NJ: Paulist Press.
- Kegan, R., & Lahey, L.L., 2009. *Immunity to Change: How to Overcome It and Unlock the Potential in Yourself and Your Organization.* Boston, MA: Harvard Business School Publishing Corporation.

- Kotter, J.P., 1985. *Power and Influence: Beyond Formal Authority.* New York: Free Press.
- Mann, D., 2015 (3rd Ed.). *Creating a Lean Culture: Tools to Sustain a Lean Conversion.* Boca Raton, FL: CRC Press.
- Maslow, A.H., 1954. *Motivation and Personality.* New York: Harper & Brothers.
- Schein, E.H., 2013. *Humble Inquiry: The Gentle Art of Asking Instead of Telling.* San Francisco, CA: Barrett-Koehler Publishers Inc.
- Weick, K.E., & Sutcliffe, K.M., 2015 (3rd Ed.). *Managing the Unexpected: Sustained Performance in a Complex World.* Hoboken, NJ: John Wiley & Sons Inc.
- Wilber, K., 2016. *Integral Meditation: Mindfulness as a Way to Grow Up, Wake Up, and Show Up in Your Life.* Boulder, CO: Shambhala Publications Inc.

Author Biographies

Aaron Fausz, PhD

For more than 25 years, Aaron has helped organizations align and improve their personnel and technical systems to accomplish strategic business objectives. Aaron has consulted with leading healthcare organizations across the country. His areas of expertise and professional skills include guiding organizations through strategically driven changes and enhancing business performance, with significant experience in needs assessment, best practice analysis, performance measurement, process improvement, and behavioral change management. He holds a Doctorate in Industrial and Organizational Psychology from the University of Tennessee in Knoxville with a minor in Industrial Engineering.

William Kirkwood, PhD

Bill has more than 35 years of leadership experience in the healthcare industry. Bill has worked in both system and individual hospital settings in the Midwest and Northeast United States, leading transformational change management initiatives. This experience includes leading service line re-design initiatives as well as serving in an executive capacity in quality, operations, and human resources. Bill's areas of expertise and professional skills include facilitating change management strategies. He serves as adjunct faculty in the University of Cincinnati's Masters in Health Administration and is a certified executive coach. Bill holds a Master in Health Administration from Xavier University and a Doctorate in Organizational Behavior from the Union Institute and University in Cincinnati, Ohio.

Blair Warman Nickle, MBA, MSLS

Blair brings more than 30 years of experience in the healthcare industry. Her areas of expertise include performance measurement and improvement methods, information systems implementation, strategic planning and deployment, and project management. Blair is also an instructional designer and master trainer, having developed numerous performance-based training programs and trained novice trainers to a high level of competency in delivering education. She has consulted with hospitals, integrated health systems, physician group practices, payers, and pharmaceutical companies across the Unites States, Canada, and Mexico. Blair holds a Master of Business Administration and Master of Science in Library and Information Science degree from the University of Tennessee, Knoxville. Her undergraduate work was done at Emory & Henry College.

Maureen Sullivan, RN, BSN

Maureen has more than 35 years of experience in healthcare. Prior to her years in consulting, Maureen filled a variety of leadership roles directing quality and Lean process improvement in a community hospital and as part of a larger health system. In addition, Maureen also held advancing leadership roles in nursing management and medical surgical nursing within a not-for-profit, teaching facility. Maureen's areas of expertise include facilitation and training of quality and strategy deployment, process improvement, and management systems including coaching of leaders at all levels of the organization. Maureen has consulted with a variety of organizations including small rural hospitals, for-profit and not-for-profit community hospitals, large academic medical systems, primary and specialty clinics, quality networks, and healthcare facility architects. Maureen received her BS degree in Nursing with a focus on Healthcare Management from Metropolitan State University in Denver, CO.

Made in the USA
Lexington, KY
25 November 2019